Migritude

Migritude

By Shailja Patel

KAYA PRESS

NEW YORK, NY

Published by Kaya Press (Muae Publishing, Inc.) www.kaya.com

Cover design and artwork by spoon+fork
Cover image © AMREF/RILEY200P
Manufactured in the United States of America

Distributed by D.A.P./Distributed Art Publishers
155 Avenue of the Americas, 2nd Floor New York, NY 10013
800.338.BOOK, www.artbook.com

ISBN: 9781885030054
Library of Congress Cataloging-in-Publication Data
Patel, Shailja.
 Migritude / by Shailja Patel.
    p. cm.
 ISBN 978-1-885030-05-4
1. Patel, Shailja. 2. Poets, American--21st century--Biography. 3. Performance
artists--United States--Biography. I. Title.
PS3616.A8665Z46 2010
813'.6--dc22
[B]   2010035260

This publication is made possible by support from the National Endowment
for the Arts and public funds from the New York State Council on the Arts, a
state agency. Additional support provided by the USC Dana and David Dornsife
College of Arts, Letters, and Sciences; the USC Department of American Studies
and Ethnicity; and the USC Asian American Studies Program. Special thanks
to the Choi Chang Soo Foundation for their support of this work. Funding
was also provided by the generous contributions of Lisa Chen & Andy Hsiao,
Floyd Cheung, Douglas Choi, Jim Chu, Susannah Donahue-Negbaur, Sesshu
Foster, Prince Gomolvilas, Thea Gray & Jeanine Mattson, Lillian Howan, Qing
Lan Huang, Keesoo Huh & Jisun Suh, Helen Kim & Stephen Lee, Juliana S. Koo
& Paul Smith, Bill Lee & Corey Ohama, Whakyung & Hong Yung Lee, Ericka
Mattuck, Minya & Yun Oh, Lily So & Tom Beischer, Duncan Williams, Amelia
Wu & Sachin Adarkar, Anita Wu & James Spicer, Amy Zeifang, and others.

NATIONAL
ENDOWMENT
FOR THE ARTS
A great nation
deserves great art.

State of the Arts

NYSCA

Kim Cook
Chandrika Patel
LD

TABLE OF CONTENTS

SPEAKING OF SARIS
by Vijay Prashad

As a schoolboy I was fascinated by the stories of
Mohenjo-Daro and Harappa, the oldest civilization
(c. 2600 B. C. E.) on the Indian subcontinent,
discovered by accident in the 1920s. A grainy picture
in my schoolbook depicted a remarkable seal with
a flat-bottomed boat and a rudder. Two large birds
stood on the boat. The script from the Indus Valley
Civilization has yet to be deciphered, but our teacher
told us what the birds might have represented:
released birds typically try to find the shortest route
to land, so the ancient mariners might have used them
for navigation.

Many years later, in the upper reaches of the University
of Chicago's Regenstein Library I chanced upon a
travelogue from a mid-19th century British imperial
tourist, Samuel Baker. In search of the source of the Nile,
the Great Prize, Baker got lost. Somewhere near what
would be named Lake Victoria, he ran into traders whose
ancestral origins were in India. Nothing was as clear as
he (or I) would have liked. The traders pointed the way,
but wanted little else to do with the British official.

Movement is trans-historical. People, not least
those from southern Asia, have made their various
pilgrimages for millennia. But there is something very
important that distinguishes those earlier movements
from those of our modern world. In the old days, people
moved; they lived in new places, or they returned to their
homes. Most rulers, so inflamed by their own sense of

superiority, cared little about whom they ruled over. Territory was what mattered to them, and the terror that they could inflict upon those who threatened their territory was what detained them. As long as tribute flowed from the people, how those people lived and what they looked like was of little consequence. Perhaps the most well-developed version of this kind of social arrangement was the Ottoman Empire's *millet* regime. It allowed for social and cultural diversity, even when this disturbed the equanimity of the sultans.

So much good has come from modernity: freedoms of the mind, and of the stomach. It is hard to look back at older ways of being with nostalgia. Things were hard in the old days. And yet, with the modern came some brutal social forms, one of which was the scientific linkage of blood to belonging. Caste and bondage has a long history, a brutal past that leaks into the uncomfortable present. Those older social oppressions are now married to the technology of the modern State, whose capacity to measure and count, to conduct surveillance and police its borders, is far more efficient than that of the pre-modern State. It is this linkage between older ideas and new technologies that makes migration of the past so different from migration of the present.

"Immigration," as a concept, is born in the era of imperialism. "Immigrants," in this context, are not just those who cross boundaries, but those who pointedly enter the advanced industrial states from lands of dusky skin. Immigration is always already about mobile capital and immobile race. Colonial rulers went where they willed, and they even moved people from one colony to another; but the colonized were not to be fully welcome in the heartlands of the empire, in Europe, in the United

States. If they came, they were allowed in for their labor, not for their lives. Those Indian traders in Africa would become foreigners, not just outsiders. Racism would overwhelm older forms of xenophobia.

It is from such histories that Shailja Patel's remarkable narrative is woven. Three cross-continental migrations shape her story: the early 20th century march of South Asians to East Africa; the mass expulsion and emigration of East African Indians to the Global North from the 1970s onwards; and finally, Shailja's own emigration out of Kenya – first to the United Kingdom and, eventually, to California.

California is a peculiarly schizophrenic place to be a migrant. On March 31, 2001, the state began to celebrate Cesar E. Chavez Day, to honor the farm worker leader and to celebrate the contribution of migrants to the state. In 2006, the U.S. Congress passed the Secure Fence Act, whose intent is to take the many physical barriers along the U.S.-Mexico border and meld them into the Great Wall of America. The Border Wall is an affront to the heritage of Chavez, and to the migrants whose labor created and continues to maintain California as we know it. It is a monument to the brutality of the U.S. war on migrants. (Operation Gatekeeper, begun in 1994, claimed the lives of 444 migrants over five years; the East German border guards killed 263 people from 1949 to 1989.)

These two visions for California are in constant combat, and it is on one side of this conflagration that Shailja decided to unpack the trousseau of saris given to her by her mother. Through them, she reveals an inheritance of emotions, of histories bound up in journeys from India to Kenya to the United States. The sari, a piece of cloth, binds continents and families. But it is also that which allows us to think of the bind: it holds things together, it bandages wounds, but it also obliges us to think about what it means to be bound together. We are as bound by the struggles of the migrant workers who have inserted their bodies and desires into our society as we are by the granite block of the power elite that is loath to cede its power or open its purse. This bind is the central metaphor of Shailja's book.

Shailja's book is not simply about migrants. It's about the condition of migration – of *migritude*. It is not a cultural anthropology of migrant lives, but rather a philosophical meditation on what it means to live within the concept of Migrant. Riffing as it does off the term *négritude*, it is also about race. Léopold Sédar Senghor caught the spirit of négritude when he wrote: "Far from seeing in one's blackness an inferiority, one accepts it, one lays claim to it with pride, one cultivates it lovingly." Senghor's friend Aime Césaire coined the term in his *Cahier d'un Retour au Pays Natal* (1939, *Notebook of a Return to My Native Land*), where he wrote that négritude is "not a cephalic index, or a plasma, or a soma, but [it is] measured by the compass of suffering."

Migritude draws from this heritage to suggest that there is a "compass of suffering" shared by migrants of color into the heartlands of power. It shows how this compass binds them in unexpected ways. The term migritude suggests the horizontal assimilation engineered by migrants as they smile at each other, knowing quite well what is carried on each other's backs.

I came to Shailja Patel's *Migritude* joyously, embraced by the first few lines about the teardrop in Babylon.

The embrace didn't falter. The words held me. They are a song. What does the song hope for? It wants understanding, which is a gesture toward freedom.

I.

Migritude

A battered red suitcase holds my trousseau – eighteen saris, collected by my mother for when I marry. Migritude is the mantra that unlocks the suitcase, that releases the saris.

The origins of this book, and the show that gave birth to it, can be traced to a benefit in San Francisco where I performed the poem "Shilling Love." After the show, a woman named Kim Cook approached me and told me she was a director. She said she had heard "something like a bell" in my work and would be happy to talk to me, no strings attached, if I wanted advice or guidance.

Kim Cook was to become Migritude's director, dramturge, and creative production partner. But nerves, uncertainty, shyness, and fear that I wasn't ready sucked up nine months before I finally called her. When we met, I told her I was considering a one-woman show. "About what?" she asked. "Empire," I said. "What else?" "The South Asian diaspora," I said. Much later, Kim told me that her internal response had been: "Yeah, yeah, every earnest young poet wants to talk about colonization and identity." Out loud, she said: "Anything else?" I replied: "Well, I have this suitcase of saris. My mother's been gathering them since I was a child, for my marriage. She finally got tired of waiting and just gave them to me." And Kim said to herself: "Now THAT'S a story."

Migritude – a 90-minute theatre show complete with set, choreography, dance, soundscape, and visuals – was born from that exchange. It has traveled the world, from San Francisco to Vienna to Zanzibar, finally reaching this incarnation as the book you are now holding.

It all began with a battered red suitcase filled with untold stories and unseen beauty.

PRELUDE

Utaavale ambe naa paake.
You cannot rush mangoes to ripeness.

—GUJARATI PROVERB

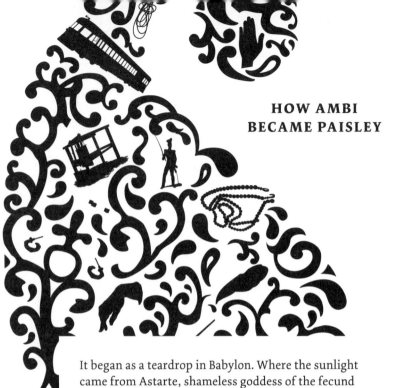

HOW AMBI
BECAME PAISLEY

It began as a teardrop in Babylon. Where the sunlight
came from Astarte, shameless goddess of the fecund
feminine. The boteh. Stylized rendition of the date-palm
shoot, tree of life, fertility symbol. It danced through
Celtic art, until the heavy feet of Roman legionaries
tramped over the Alps. Then it fled the rage of Mars and
Jupiter, dove underground as Empire rose.

Some historians claim it travelled to Mughal courts
from Victorian England as the foliaged shape of a herbal.
Evolved into a cone, then a tadpole. But a legend in
Kashmir calls it the footprint of the goddess Parvati. As
she ran through the Himalayas at the dawn of time.

Ambi. Form of a mango. Fruit that ripens
and rots in the dreams of all South-to-North
immigrants. A shape like a peacock feather.

Like half a heart, sliced on a smooth s-shaped curve. Something that would feel good in the hand: round to the palm like a solid breast, narrow to a sharp point to test the pad of the finger. An image a child could draw, single stroke, free form, and still produce something elegant.

Have you ever sliced a heart on a curve? Which piece would you keep?

There was a craft of weavers. Makers of mosuleen, named after its city of origin, Mosul, in Iraq. A fabric so fine, you could fit a thirty-yard length of it into a matchbox. Egyptian pharaohs used it to wrap mummies. Imperial Rome imported it for women of nobility to drape, seductively, around their bodies. Two Indian cities rose to glory and fame on the waves of mosuleen: Masulipatnam in South India and Dhaka in Bengal.

Enter the Barbarian. Imperialism. Armed with a switchblade, designed to slice the heart out of craft. To separate makers from the fruits of their labor. To stab the mangoes out of their hands. In 1813, Dhaka mosuleen sold at a 75% profit on the London market, yet was still cheaper than local British fabric. The British weighed it down with an 80% duty. But that wasn't enough. They needed to force India to buy British cloth. So down the alleyways of Dhaka stamped the legionaries – British, this time, not Roman. Hunted down the terrified weavers, chopped off their index fingers and thumbs.

How many ways can you clone an empire? Dice a people, digit by digit?

In 1846, Britain annexed the vale of Kashmir, fabled paradise of beauty, and sold it to Maharaj Gulab Singh of

Jammu for one million pounds.

How do you price a country? How do you value its mountains and lakes, the scent of its trees, the colors of its sunset? What's the markup on the shapes of fruit in the dreams of its people?

Article Ten from the Treaty of Amritsar, 1846:

> *Maharaj Gulab Singh acknowledges the supremacy*
> *of the British Government, and will, in token of such*
> *supremacy, present annually to the British Government:*
> *- One horse*
> *- 12 shawl goats of approved breed (6 male and 6 female)*
> *- Three pairs of Cashmere shawls*

Kashmiri shawls. Woven on handlooms, patterned with ambi, rich and soft and intricate as mist over Kashmir's terrace gardens. First taken to Britain by bandits – known also as "merchants" – in the employ of the British East India Company, they wove their way through the dreams of Victorian wives like the footprint of a goddess no one dared imagine.

Has your skin ever craved a texture you could not name? Have you ever held strange cloth to your cheek and felt your heart thud?

There was a village in Scotland. Paisley. A tiny town of weavers who became known as radical labor agitators. Weaving offers too much time for dangerous talk. Weavers of Paisley learned how to churn out imitation ambi, on imitation Kashmiri shawls, and got to keep their index fingers and thumbs.

Until Kashmiri became cashmere. Mosuleen became muslin. Ambi became paisley.

And a hundred and fifty years later, chai became a beverage invented in California.

How many ways can you splice a history? Price a country? Dice a people? Slice a heart? Entice what's been erased back into story? My-gritude.

Have you ever taken a word in your hand, dared to shape your palm to the hollow where the fullness falls away? Have you ever pointed it back to its beginning? Felt it leap and shudder in your fingers like a dowsing rod? Jerk like a severed thumb? Flare with the forbidden name of a goddess returning? My-gritude.

Have you ever set out to search for a missing half? The piece that isn't shapely, elegant, simple. The half that's ugly, heavy, abrasive. Awkward to the hand. Gritty on the tongue.

Migritude.

PART I: Nairobi, Kenya
1972 – 1989

Raat thodi ne vesh jaja.
The night is short and our garments change.

——GUJARATI PROVERB

1. IDI AMIN

In 1972, Idi Amin, military dictator of Uganda, expelled the country's entire Asian population.

I was born and raised in Kenya. The country bordering Uganda.

Third-generation East African Asian.

Raat thodi ne vesh jaja, the proverb I grew up on. *The night is short and our garments change.*

Meaning: Don't put down roots. Don't get too comfortable. By dawn, we may be on the move, forced to reinvent ourselves in order to survive. Invest only in what we can carry. Passports. Education. Jewellery.

In olden days, my mother says, *they didn't have banks,*

so they invested in jewellery. The women would carry the
family's savings in their gold ornaments, their valuable saris.
It was safest – and you see, it kept them safe. Women were
respected, because they wore and guarded the family's wealth.

I grew up on tales of the last trains
coming out of Uganda. Laden with
traumatized Asians who had been
stripped of all they possessed. The
grown-ups whispered: *They took even the*
wedding rings, the earrings, off the women.
They searched their hair.

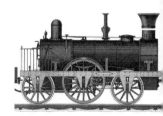

Image that haunted my childhood: a man on Nairobi's
railway platform who held his toddler child and cried.
Cried aloud, through a wide-open mouth. Soldiers had
boarded the train just outside Kampala, had dragged
his wife off while he watched. Too terrified for the child
on his lap to resist. The carriage filled with mute, numb
people. He cried now because there was nothing left to
hold tears back for. Not dignity. Not manhood. Not hope.

Her jewellery did not protect her.

Secret documents, declassified in 2001, show that
Britain, Israel, and the US instigated and backed
Idi Amin's military coup, which overthrew Uganda's
democratically elected government. What followed
were eight years of terror that devastated Uganda,
left hundreds of thousands dead. British Foreign
Office documents describe Idi Amin as *a man we can*
do business with.

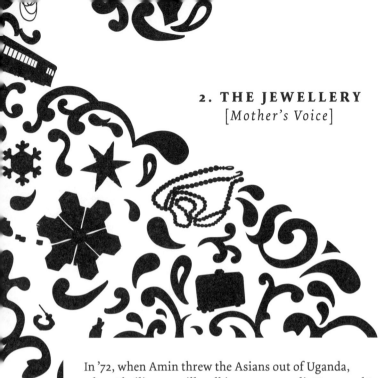

2. THE JEWELLERY
[*Mother's Voice*]

In '72, when Amin threw the Asians out of Uganda, when Shailja was still walking pa-pa-pugli, Naree and I made the trip to England in winter with all my valuable jewellery from my trousseau to put safely in Midland Bank for the daughters.

We carried the jewellery right inside our coats, through customs and immigration. Thank god they didn't stop us at the airports. At Nairobi airport, they would have just taken it. At Heathrow, they would have made us pay duty.

It was so cold, you can't imagine. We took the bus and the Tube everywhere, carrying the jewellery. Their father put some in his inside pocket. I put the rest in my bag, and I carried my bag in front of me, like this, so no one could take it.

We never let go for one second until we were in the vault down inside the bank. We put the jewellery into the safe deposit box, and I wrote everything down. I checked the list twice. We put the key in the envelope, the one they keep there, and they sealed it and made us sign over the seal, both of us, so no one else could open it. Then we felt as if a weight had lifted and we could both breathe. We were so relieved. Their father said:

Aaah. Now let's go and have a hot cup of tea.

We went to a restaurant, Naree and me and my brother Vinod, and we had tea. They served it to us cold. You know the way the English put cold milk in their tea. But for once we didn't mind. You can't imagine how scared we were when the trains came from Uganda with the Asians on them crying, asking for milk for their children. They were literally thrown out with nothing.

On the way home, when we were standing on the railway platform, I started to cry. My jewellery was gone. I would never wear it again. Even the smallest pieces, the ones I used to love putting on you children, and everyone would say how pretty you looked. All locked up, in that dark vault.

I wrote down the details of each set. *Heavy gold set: necklace, earrings, four bangles, ring inset with diamonds. Green set: necklace, earrings, bracelet, nathni.* In Gujarati, so the dhorias and karias couldn't read it. I wrote the list twice. I put one in the safe deposit box and kept the other with me. I kept that list in my handbag

everywhere I went in the UK, and I never put my handbag down for a second. I tried to train my daughters that way: You never let your bag out of your sight.

[SHAILJA's voice, exasperated]: Mummy, don't be so paranoid. We're in someone's home! No one is going to steal your bag.

Ha! What do they know? People can be nasty and evil. My daughters have never known real hardship; they think everything can be replaced. They don't know how to take care of things.

Every time I went to the UK – it was always my fate to make winter journeys, even though I hated traveling in the winter – I went to check on the safe deposit box. In '77, when my father was ill in London, I took all three children with me. Can you imagine, making that journey from Kenya to England with three little girls? Shruti was nine. She stayed at my parents' house in London with Sneha, who was only three. I took Shailja with me everywhere I went. Each time I visited the bank, I would take my list in my handbag and check every single item. Even if it's a bank, you have to keep an eye on things. And I added new pieces – my mother's pieces that came to me when she died.

When we sent Shruti to the UK, I told her:

First and foremost, make sure your uncle has paid the yearly fee for the safe deposit box.

3. HISTORY LESSON

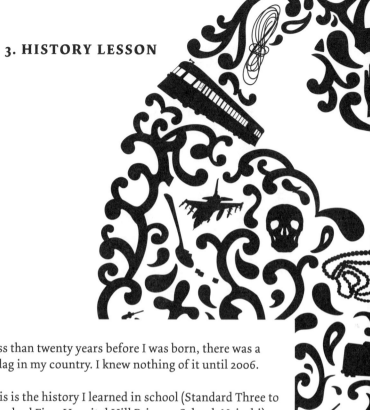

Less than twenty years before I was born, there was a gulag in my country. I knew nothing of it until 2006.

This is the history I learned in school (Standard Three to Standard Five, Hospital Hill Primary School, Nairobi).

> The first man and first woman were Gikuyu and Mumbi. They gave birth to the nine clans of the Kikuyu. The Mugwe was the leader who parted the waters, long before Moses, and led his people to freedom. Koitalel arap Samoei predicted the coming of the white man and the railway (a long snake, spitting fire). He led the Nandi people against the first British invaders. Waiyaki wa Hinga, paramount chief, went unarmed to a supposedly friendly meeting with British Officer Purkiss. He was killed!

We scribbled *Purkiss Pig-Face* into the margins of our textbook. We burned with the righteous outrage of nine-year-olds.

We sang about the Maji Maji uprising in Tanzania to the tune of Boney M's "Rivers of Babylon."

By the rivers of Rufiji
To Mahenge Plateau
Hey hey we'll win
When we drive out the Germans!
Maji Maji!

Sprinkle maize, millet, and water!
Protect us from German guns!
We're fighting for independence
For our daughters and sons!
Maji Maji!

Maji Maji. Where Africans went into battle against the German military armed with spears, bows, and arrows. They believed that a magic brew of maize, millet, and water would offer bullet-proof protection. They were slaughtered.

We sang about Shaka the Zulu king to the tune of "My Favourite Things."

Shaka the Zulu, he was a great leader
Fought with his impis with shields of two meters
Short stabbing spears his men used to fight
That's how his army gained all of their might...

This is the history we didn't learn.

From 1952 to 1960, the people of Kenya mounted a fierce guerilla struggle, the Mau Mau uprising, to reclaim their land and freedom from the British. The British incarcerated, tortured, and murdered approximately 25,000 Kenyans. Men, women, and children. More than a million Kenyans were detained for over eight years in concentration camps – barbed wire villages where forced labour, starvation, and death were routine.

This is the history we read in school.

President Jomo Kenyatta's speech, ten months after Kenya's independence:

Let this be the day on which all of us commit ourselves to erase from our minds all the hatreds and the difficulties of those years which now belong to history. Let us agree that we shall never refer to the past. Let us instead unite, in all our utterances and activities, in concern for the reconstruction of our country and the vitality of Kenya's future.

This is the history we didn't read.

Oral testimonies from women who survived the camps:

The white officers had no shame. They would rape women in full view of everyone. Swing women by the hair. Put women in sacks, douse in paraffin, set alight.

They burned us with cigarette butts. Forced us to walk on hot coals.

They put cayenne pepper and water in our vaginas.
Petrol and water in our vaginas. Forced in with a bottle
pushed by a boot.

You were forced to work even if your children were sick.
If you had a sick baby, you strapped it to your back while
you worked. The home guards would beat you if you
stopped to attend to it. You would finally bring the child
around to check on it, and find it was dead. You would
start screaming in shock and anguish. The home guards
would order the others to come and help you bury it.

Every morning when the barracks were opened, the
homeguards would ask:

How many children have died?

They would be tied in bundles of six babies. Each of us
would be ordered to take a bundle and bury it with the
rest of the bodies in the graves.

In April 1956, Britain's *Sunday Post* ran an interview with
Katherine Warren-Gash, the officer in charge of Kamiti
women's camp. She said:

Confession and "rehabilitation" of women in the camp
is proving better than a course of beauty treatment! The
women arrive sullen, sour, unpleasant, downright ugly.
But after confession and rehabilitation, many of them
become really pretty.

We learned in school that we attained independence
peacefully.

Without bloodshed.

We were the model the rest of Africa was supposed to look to! A happy, multiracial nation where Whites, Asians, and Africans all lived in harmony.

In Kenya's war of independence, fewer than 100 whites and over 25,000 Africans died. Half of the Africans who died were children under ten.

Sixty thousand white settlers lived in Kenya at independence in 1963. The new Kenyan government was required to take loans of 12.5 million pounds from its ex-colonial master, the British government. To buy back stolen land from settlers who wished to leave.

4. SWORE I'D NEVER WEAR CLOTHES I COULDN'T RUN OR FIGHT IN

The Hindu epic, the Mahabharata says:

That is a well-governed state where a woman, adorned with all dress and ornaments, and unaccompanied by men, can move freely and fearlessly in its roads and lanes.

Since the US invaded Iraq, thousands of Iraqi women and girls have been abducted. Vanished. A phenomenon unknown under Saddam Hussein. When societies are blown apart, women become prey.

Looking pretty, my mother said, *is the least you can do. Looking pretty is the least you can do, Shailja, to make up for not being a boy.*

You are not safe as a girl, my mother said. *If you had a brother to protect you, you could go out at night. If you had a brother to protect you, we would let you.*

But how could I run if a man attacked me and I was wearing a sari? How would I fight?

As a child, I knew of women strangled in their saris. Women doused in paraffin and burned in their saris. Saris made you vulnerable. A walking target. Saris made you weak.

No one told me about women who went into battle – in their saris.

Worked the fields – in their saris.

Why didn't anyone tell me about women who laboured on construction sites in their saris?

All I heard was:

You have to be careful in a sari. You're exposing (whisper) *the body. Don't let the pallav slip under the breast. That's obscene. Don't let the petticoat show the panties. That's obscene. Allure without being sexual. Be beautiful without being aware of it. Attract without meeting anyone's eyes.*

You must never act as if you owned your body. It's draped and displayed for the edification of others. Watch the women in Bollywood movies! Combine coy virginality with hip-swinging sex appeal.

As a child, I swore I would never wear clothes I couldn't run or fight in. My legs would never be hobbled.

5. I NEVER WANTED DAUGHTERS
[*Mother's Voice*]

Three times in my life I've sliced my heart open on an S-shaped curve. The first was Shruti – the child they told me I would never have. Shruti means "divine revelation." And she was. Our gift from Mataji.

Then Shailja. Named for Parvati, the flowering of stone in temples, the cave paintings of the goddess in Sri Lanka. No wonder she became an artist.

Finally, Sneha. Beloved.

You never forget the pain of childbirth. It's something no one can imagine. Your heart is never whole again once you have a daughter.

I never wanted daughters. Women are never safe. My daughters make me so angry! They keep seeking out

danger. After everything we've done for their security, they reject us. They choose the hardest, worst, most dangerous things.

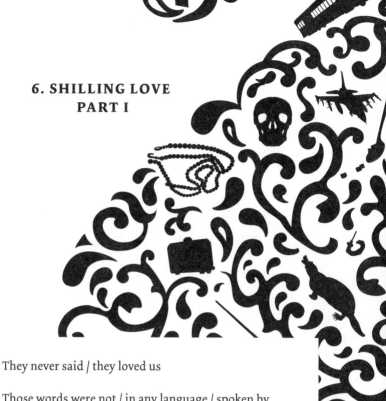

6. SHILLING LOVE
PART I

They never said / they loved us

Those words were not / in any language / spoken by
my parents

I love you honey / was the dribbled caramel / of Hollywood
movies / *Dallas* / *Dynasty* / where electricity surged
through skyscrapers / twenty-four hours a day / hot
water gushed / at the touch of gleaming taps / banquets
obscene as the Pentagon / were mere backdrops / to
emotions without consequences / words that / cost
nothing / meant nothing / would never have to be
redeemed

My parents / didn't speak / that language

1975 / fifteen Kenyan shillings to the British pound / my

mother speaks battle / storms the bastions of Nairobi's /
most exclusive prep schools / hurls / our cowering,
six-year-old bodies / like cannonballs / into all-white
classrooms / scales the ramparts / of class distinction
around Loreto Convent / where the president / sends
his daughter / where foreign diplomats / send their
daughters / because / my mother's daughters / will /
have / world-class educations

she falls / re-groups / falls and
re-groups / in endless assaults on
visa officials / who sneer behind
bullet-proof windows / at British
and US consulates

my mother / the general / arms
her daughters / to take on every
citadel

1977 / twenty Kenyan shillings to the British pound / my
father speaks stoic endurance / he began at sixteen / the
brutal apprenticeship / of a man who takes care of his
own / dreams / of pilot / rally driver / relinquished / to
the daily crucifixion / of wringing profits / from beneath
cars / my father / the foot soldier / bound to an honour /
deeper than any currency

*you must / finish what you start you must / march until you
drop you must / give your life for those / you bring into the world*

I try to explain love / in shillings / to those who've / never
gauged who gets to leave / who has to stay / who breaks
free / and what they pay / those who've never counted
love / in every rung of the ladder / from survival / to
choice / a force as grim and determined / as a boot up

the backside / a spur that draws blood / a mountaineer's rope / that yanks / relentlessly / up

My parents never say / they love us / they save and count / count and save

The shilling falls against the pound / college fees for overseas students / rise like flood tides / love is a luxury / priced in hard currency / ringed by tariffs / and we on the raft / devour prospectuses of ivied buildings / smooth lawns / vast libraries / gleaming science labs / the way Jehovah's Witnesses / gobble visions of paradise / because we know we'll have to be / twice as good / three times as fast / four times as driven / with angels / powers / and principalities on our side / just / to get / on the plane

Thirty shillings to the pound / forty shillings to the pound / my parents fight over money / late in the night my father / pounds the walls and yells / *I can't* / *it's impossible* / *what do you think I am?*

My mother propels us through / tutors, exams, scholarship applications / locks us into rooms to study / keeps an iron grip / on the bank books

1982 / gunshots in the streets of Nairobi / military coup leaders / thunder over the radio / Asian businesses wrecked and looted / Asian women / raped / after the government / regains control / we whisper what the coup leaders / had planned

Round up all the Asians / at gunpoint / in the national stadium / strip them of what they carry / march them fifty kilometres to the airport / elders in wheelchairs / babies in arms / pack them onto foreign planes / like

battery chickens / tell the pilots down rifle barrels /
leave / we don't care where you take them / leave

I learn / like a stone in my gut / that third-generation
Asian Kenyan / will never / be Kenyan enough / that all
my patriotic fervour / will not / turn my skin / black

As yet another western country / drops a portcullis of
immigration spikes / my mother straps my shoulders
back with a belt / to teach me / *stand up straight*

Fifty shillings to the pound / we cry over meltdown
pressure / of exam after exam / where second place is
never good enough

They snap / their faces taut with fear / *you can't be soft /*
you must be strong / you have to fight / or the world will eat
you up

Seventy shillings to the pound / they hug us at airports /
tearless / stoic / as we board planes for icy / alien England /
cram instructions into our pockets like talismans

eat proper meals / so you don't get sick / cover your ears /
against the cold / stay away from the muffathias / the ones
without purpose or values / learn and study / succeed / learn
and study / succeed / remember remember remember / the cost
of your life

they never say / they love us

PART II: United Kingdom and United States 1990 – 2004

Jagia tyanthi savar.
Whenever you wake up, that's when your morning begins.

—GUJARATI PROVERB

7. THE MAKING (MIGRANT SONG)

*Make it out of the sari that wraps you / in tender celebration /
like the mother you longed for / make it out of the mother you
got / in all her wounded magnificence*

*Make it out of every scar and callus / on your father's hands /
and how you always wanted / tough mechanic's hands like
his / credentialled by each ground-down / fingernail each /
palm line seamed with grease*

*Distill it from the offering / of his hands / to fifty years of
labor / to guarantee that his daughters / would never have to
work with theirs*

Make it / to find out / what your own hands are good for

A friend once gave my parents a scratched old Skeeter Davis record. They loved it. The lyrics captured all their favorite convictions. *Only The Strong Survive. I Didn't Cry Today. I'm Gonna Join The Family Circle Once Again.* They hummed the tunes for weeks.

Country western is perfect migrant music. Hardship, loss, suffering, all wrapped up in saccharine sentimentality to make it bearable.

We overdress, we migrants. We care too much how we look to you. We get it wrong. We ought to look like we don't give a fuck. We show up ridiculously groomed, bearing elaborate gifts. We are too formally grateful.

We cringe in silent shame for you when you don't offer food or drink. Eat before us without sharing. Serve yourselves first. Insult us without knowing.

Two white Americans said to me, when I shared my doughnut with them:

We've never seen anyone cut a doughnut into three pieces.

We calibrate hunger precisely. Define enough differently from you. Enough is what's available, shared between everyone present. We are incapable of saying, as you can so easily:

Sorry, there's not enough for you.

We absorb information without asking questions. Questions cost us jobs, visas, lives. We watch and copy. We try to please.

We hold back in conversations. We don't contradict so we don't show you up. You mistake this for a lack of intellectual confidence.

How much we can do without is our strength. But you find it comic. Pitiable. Miserly. You *just can't imagine* how a family of eight lives in a one-room apartment. You *don't want to think* how someone survives on $7 an hour. It makes you uncomfortable when we eat stems and peels. Dry our clothes in the sun. Repair instead of replace. You mistake austerity, living without waste, for deprivation.

It's our job to protect you from the discomfort of seeing inequality. To cushion your sense of cosmopolitan hipness when you hang out with us. Without ever challenging you too far.

We admire your $65 dollar haircut when you pay us $22 a day to raise your child. We love your children, when their strollers cost more than a year's rent where we come from. We turn away when they throw food around like another toy. To hide our tears at images we carry of children fighting over half a banana. Children picking grains of rice off the floor.

We recoil when you joke about how your kids will do social justice work in Palestine as teenagers. As if Palestine will never be anything but a social justice summer camp. A case study in genocidal oppression for wealthy American teens with wanna-be-radical parents.

We suck it up when you ask if your children can touch our hair, our skin, our clothes. As if we were wax models.

I had a housemate who offered me her heavily used
bedding when she left.

*It's worn out and dirty, I was going to throw it out. But you
often find uses for things I toss, so I'm appealing to your sense
of parsimony.*

A man I once dated, an award-winning Israeli filmmaker
of social justice documentaries, gave me a broken lamp
as a housewarming gift. *I know you fix things*, he said.

*So I make this work from rage / for every smug, idiotic face
I've ever wanted to smash into the carnage of war / every
encounter that's left my throat choked / with what I dared
not say / I excavate the words that hid in my churning
stomach through visa controls / words I swallowed down
until over the border / they are still there / they knew I would
come back for them*

*This is for the hands / hacked off the
Arawaks by Columbus and his men /
lopped off Ohlone children by Spanish
priests / baskets of severed hands
presented at day's end / to Belgian
plantation masters in the Congo /
thumbs chopped off Indian weavers by
the British*

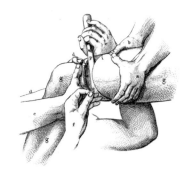

*I make this work / because I still
have hands*

Israeli soldiers shot and killed a nine-year-old girl in the Gaza strip. *She was carrying a large bag and ignored warning shots.*

What's the protocol for a nine-year-old in response to warning shots?

But I can't say that Israel is the apartheid South Africa of our times. The only country in the world whose constitution allows torture.

Why does the word "Islamic" always precede the word "terrorist" when the word "Catholic" never precedes the word "Nazi"? And why has the Catholic Church never excommunicated Hitler?

Meanwhile, Pepsi buys up water rights in Central Africa, but keeps the water dirty, except for what it bottles to sell back to those who live there.

I want the gutters of Berkeley to float plastic bottles, like the ditches of Nairobi. I want the poodles of New York to choke on plastic bags like the cows and goats of Zanzibar.

"The Lion Sleeps Tonight" grosses fifteen million dollars worldwide while South African Solomon Linda, who wrote the song, gets one dollar for the copyright and dies at fifty-three from poverty.

Yes, I'm exploding. Like the internal organs of four hundred dolphins sonar-blasted to death in the Indian Ocean by the US Navy.

Yes, I'm outta control, like the billions of dollars Africa

pays each year to the global North. For debt incurred by colonial regimes and military dictators, debt inherited by newly independent African nations.

Someone comes into your home. Evicts you at gunpoint. Occupies your property. Mortgages it three times over. To banks who know they're lending to thieves. Should you repay that debt? With penalties, late charges, 14% interest?

We all love to see bodies from Africa that move. We all love to move our bodies to rhythms from Africa. But we are terrified of African bodies that speak.

Here's how Empire stokes itself:
A Ugandan farmer earns two hundred shillings for a kilo of coffee beans. A cup of coffee at your nearest cafe sells for five thousand Uganda shillings.

Here's how Empire congratulates itself:

Favourite American torture technique: blast Metallica music at victims until they scream, weep, lose bladder and bowel control. Metallica's James Hetfield is *proud that my music is culturally offensive. If they're not used to freedom, I'm glad to be a part of the exposure.*

So I make it out of every scar and callus / on my father's hands / and how I always wanted / tough mechanic's hands like his / credentialled by each / ground-down fingernail each palm-line seamed with grease

I distill it from the offering of his hands / to fifty years of labour to guarantee / that his daughters would never / have to work with theirs

I make it to find out / what my own hands are good for

I make it out of the sari that wraps me in tender celebration / like the mother I rediscover

I make it out of the mother I got / in all her wounded magnificence

8. UNDER AND OVER

You ask me: *What goes under a sari? What does a woman wear over her saris to match their splendour?*

When I turned twenty-one, I was a student in England. At York, in the North. My sister Shruti was a medical student in Bristol, down in the South. Six hours away by coach.

We were both poor. Converted pounds to shillings in our heads. Worked the lowest paying jobs on campus because as overseas students, we weren't legally allowed to work at anything else.

I had a job interview in London a month after my twenty-first birthday. Shruti took the coach from Bristol to see me. We met up at King's Cross Station. We went to a nearby hotel for tea.

The waiters looked at us disdainfully. Two Pakis. In heavy, ugly coats. Cheap trousers. Thick sneakers for trudging through winter streets.

We thought they were going to say, *Sorry ladies. We only do teas for hotel guests.* But they let us in. Grudgingly.

Shruti gave me my twenty-first birthday present. A pure wool scarlet cape that hung down to my knees. Sleeves like wings. A wide soft collar that wrapped around my neck. It was magnificent. It was grander, more luxurious, than anything I'd ever worn before. It came from Harrods. The House of Fraser. It cost fifty pounds.

Fifty pounds?

Fifty pounds was twenty-five hours of scraping dishes, loading washers in the college kitchens. A month's salary for an office worker in Nairobi.

Fifty pounds worth of scarlet wool was my sister saying to me: *I see you. I believe in you. You shine.*

I wore that coat to every job interview after that. I've worn it over my saris even when it didn't match. I stroked it at two in the morning while studying for professional exams. Lonely, desperate, terrified I wouldn't make it.

I didn't. I failed my final exams. I lost my job and work permit. I burned all my boats. I went to America.

We migrants lie to those we love about our success. About our happiness. We tell them how wonderful things are, even when we're failing. We cannot bear to fall short of their hopes for us. To stab them with the realization that their dreams will not come true. We carry the visions of whole peoples right against our skin. We push ourselves to the breaking point to manifest them.

What we wear under our saris is unachievable perfectionism. Pride so fierce it threatens to incinerate us. We don't start anything we will not finish. We don't stop until we're done.

When I arrived in America, my eldest aunt said to me:

The first thing you say when a man approaches you is I Have Family. Everywhere. All Around. *Then he won't think you're unprotected. Try to take advantage of you.*

I have been unprotected. I have been naked and exposed. I have been clothed and armoured. I know what I carry in my suitcase. I carry my history. I carry my family. Over my saris, I wear my sisters.

9. AUSTRALIA [*Mother's Voice*]

Dearest Shailja,

Received both your envelopes with photos and notes. Thank you. We are very pleased about your latest poem, which has earned so much acclaim over radio, mass media, and at the university. We are extremely proud of your talent and brilliance! Congratulations too on the job offer at the Buddhist foundation. May you keep climbing the ladder of success and stay at the top always! I love the photo you sent of you and Shruti sitting on the steps of the hut on the mountain! It's so natural and beautiful, the way you two used to be as little girls.

Remember, dear daughters: "Charity begins at Home!" You are worried about the conflict going on in the world. But if every sensible human being lived in love and peace and stopped warring in the home, then hands would not raise to kill or hurt another human being! We cannot worry about the whole world – that is God's job! But we can do our own duty by ourselves and our family, people we love and live with and care about! That is why God created the Family Order. It is your duty to God to remain cheerful and thankful to him for what you have because He has given it all to you for your good "Karma" in your last birth.

We are fine and surviving as well as one can in the present, politically insecure climate here. We simply tend to ignore the situation and keep on living our daily lives! On Saturday, we saw a film called *Mere Yaar Ki Shadi*, meaning *My Friend's Wedding*. It was very modern and entertaining, also dubbed in English, so you'll enjoy it.

Time seems to fly. This August, we'll have been in this maisonette for twelve years! If I can help it, I would never want to migrate, but who has seen the future?! At least, we are very happy that we've sent all of you out of Kenya and settled you in the UK and America; we see other parents frantic with worry for their children now. They have only one road open to them: Australia! All young Asians are heading towards this country and trying to settle there. As people leave, there are the farewell dinners and parties, gifts to be wrapped and delivered as momentos, a little cry as each family leaves; but then, that is LIFE isn't it?!

You must take everything of yours the next time you come – papers, certificates, documents, clothes, saris, etc. Take care, bete.

Bye,
Mummy

10. THE SKY HAS NOT CHANGED COLOUR

*Blood is red. The land is red. The sky was red the day they
found me – and did what they did. The skin of the child I bore
was red. Then it turned pale yellow, like urine. Like a sick
plant. How can there be a god who allows such things
to happen?*

In 2002, the stories began to filter into the press. Local
papers first, then international. British soldiers, posted
to Kenya for military training, had raped hundreds of
Kenyan women. To date, over 650 rape allegations have
been made. More than half the cases involve gang rape.
Some of those assaulted were children at the time. The
allegations cover 35 years, from 1965 (just two years after
Kenya won independence from Britain) to 2001.

They are the noble savages, staring out from coffee table books. *Africa Adorned*. *The Last Nomads*. Backdrops and extras for *Vogue* fashion shoots. Stock ingredients for tourist brochures. The Maasai are a global brand. The sun sets behind them, glints through the huge holes in their earlobes. They are the myth of tribal splendour. Everything about them is foreign, exotic: shaved heads, giant beaded necklaces, bare breasts.

They roam the savannah. Hunt lions with spears. The men leap several feet in the air in tribal dances. The women ululate. They drink brews of milk and cow's blood, believe that god made three races – the blacks, the whites, and the Maasai. That all the cattle in the world belong to them. Their "timeless culture" is the stuff of children's books, of Western fantasies. They are everyone's dream of a people untouched by modernity.

Survivor 1

> Walked ten kilometres from her cousin's home to find a well that had not dried up. Three soldiers

approached her as she filled her water cans. She greeted them in English. She had just finished high school, was about to become a law student. Two soldiers raped her, while the third held their guns. After the attack, she walked the ten kilometres back to her cousin's house. Without the cans.

When she found she was pregnant, her family was outraged. They had invested everything in her education. Her labour was agonizing. She was taken to hospital for a c-section. She gave birth to twins, but one, a boy, died during labour.

She is now a school teacher. Never married. Feels grief and rage over her shattered ambitions. Deep pain and ambivalence towards her daughter, whom other children call *mzungu*.

She still wonders if they attacked her because she greeted them in English. The language that was supposed to be her key to the world.

Survivor 58

Attacked by four soldiers while herding her goats. When she saw them approach, she began to run, as it was widely known that they raped women. They chased her for over three kilometres and finally caught her. They argued about who would rape her first. She was heavily pregnant with her first child. She went into labour the next day and gave birth to a stillborn child. She told only her husband about the ordeal.

Survivor 613

Was in his early teens. While he tended his father's cattle, four soldiers approached him. One offered him a packet of biscuits, and as he reached for them, grabbed him, held him. He remembers being raped by three soldiers before he lost consciousness.

He knows of other boys who were also raped, but are too ashamed to speak of it.

Local chiefs made repeated protests to the British Army authorities. The British Army did nothing. For over two decades. Turned a blind eye while their soldiers roamed the land, assaulting women and children at will. Turned a blind eye while entire communities lived in fear.

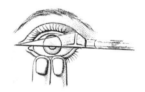

International tribunals have confirmed that rape is a form of torture.

May the redness overtake them. May red ants feast in their groins. Scorpions nestle in their beds. Blood vessels explode in their brains, organs rupture in their bellies. Wherever they go, may the land rise up in redness against them. Poison their waking and sleeping. Their walking and breathing. Their eating and drinking and shitting. May they never escape the redness on their hands. On their dicks. The bitter nausea of it on their tongues. The haze of it before their eyes, the drum of it in their ears.

Adrian Blomfield in Nanyuki reports:

Human rights activists have encouraged Kenyan prostitutes to submit fake rape claims against British soldiers.

11. MAASAI WOMEN RIOTING
[Mother's Voice]

Dearest Shailja,

Received your letter of 9th June. We are very pleased to know that you are really and seriously working towards buying your own property!

I was going to meet a friend for lunch today. But the road to her house was blocked by Maasai women rioting outside the British High Commission. They say they were molested by British soldiers. The security situation has deteriorated so badly these days, you don't feel safe going out of your house. I long for the days when we didn't need all these gates and askaris and fences!

Later I shall go for a walk and buy Shruti and Em an anniversary card. Six whole years have passed since they got married. I had hoped that by this time you two would have settled down with your husbands so Daddy and I could wind up and set off to the jungles to live on berries and fruit! Actually, I just rang him up to buy new plastic furniture for the verandah! But I can assure you, when we do go off to the forest, we shall certainly carry our sunbeds with us! And the rajais and pillows and gas cooker! So we can come back to civilization every time we run out of gas!

Bye, bete.

Love to both of you,
Mummy

12. DREAMING IN GUJARATI

The children in my dreams
speak in Gujarati
turn their trusting faces to the sun
say to me

care for us nurture us

in my dreams I shudder and I run.

I am six
in a playground of white children

Darkie, sing us an Indian song!

Eight
in a roomful of elders
all mock my broken Gujarati

English girl!

Twelve
I tunnel into books
forge an armor of English words.

Eighteen. Shaved head,
combat boots. Shamed
by grannies in white saris,
neon judgments
singe my western head.

Mother tongue

Matrubhasha

Tongue of the mother
I murder in myself

Through the years, I watch Gujarati
swell the swaggering egos of men,
mirror them over and over
at twice their natural size.

Dissolve the bones and teeth of women,
break them on anvils of duty and service,
burn them to skeletal ash.

Words that don't exist in Gujarati:

> *Self-expression*
> *Individual*
> *Lesbian*

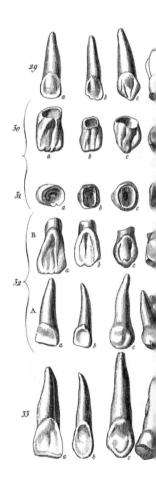

English rises in my throat,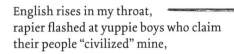
rapier flashed at yuppie boys who claim
their people "civilized" mine,

thunderbolt hurled
at cabdrivers who yell
Dirty black bastard!

force-field against
teenage hoods hissing
Fucking Paki bitch!

Their tongue – or mine?
Have I become the enemy?

Listen:
my father speaks Urdu,
language of dancing peacocks,
rosewater fountains –
even its curses are beautiful.
He speaks Hindi,
suave and melodic,
earthy Punjabi,
salty-rich as saag paneer,
coastal Swahili laced with Arabic.
He speaks Gujarati,
solid ancestral pride.

Five languages,
five different worlds.
Yet English
shrinks
him
down
before white men

who think their flat, cold spiky words
make the only reality.

Words that don't exist in English:

>	*Najjar*
>	*Garba*
>	*Arati*

If we cannot name it, does it exist?
What becomes of a tongue of
milk-heavy cows, earthen
pots, jingling anklets,
temple bells,
when its children grow up
in Silicon Valley? To be
programmers?

Then there's American:

Kin'uh get some service?

Dontcha have ice?

Not:
May I have, please?
Ben, mane madhath karso?
Tafadhali nipe rafiki
Donnez-moi, s'il vous plait
Puedo tener...

Hello, I said can I get some service?!
Like, where's the line for Ay-mericans
in this gaddamn airport?

Words that atomized 200,000 Iraqis:

Didja see how we kicked some major ass in the Gulf?
Lit up Bagdad like the fourth a' July!
Whupped those sand-niggers in'nu a parking lot!

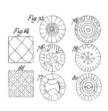

The children in my dreams speak
in Gujarati. Bright as butter, succulent
cherries, sounds I can paint on the air
with my breath, dance
through like a Sufi mystic.
Words I can weep and howl
and devour, words I can kiss
and taste and dream –
this tongue
I take
back.

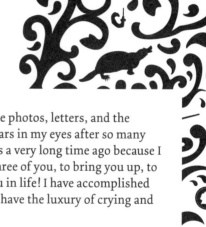

13. DAD'S VISA
[Mother's Voice]

Thank you so much for the photos, letters, and the poem, which produced tears in my eyes after so many years! I had dried my tears a very long time ago because I had to be strong for the three of you, to bring you up, to educate you and settle you in life! I have accomplished all that now. Finally, I can have the luxury of crying and feeling for myself!

Daddy still has not received his visa to travel to the US. He stood for four hours, from noon in the hot sun to 4 pm, and went back without his papers and passport. They don't even let people into the American Embassy now. They have soldiers at the entrance with guns, and they make everyone line up outside. And after all the hoo-ha with the Maasai women, the British Consulate has also erected a huge wall around its offices, with askaris at the gates. At this rate, I'm beginning to wonder if we'll even make it to London, let alone America.

15. SHILLING LOVE
PART II

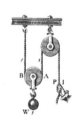

I watch how I love / I admonish / exhort / like a Himalayan guide / I rope my chosen ones / yank them remorselessly up / when they don't / even want to / be on the frigging mountain

Like a vigilante squad / I scan dark streets for threats / strategize for war and famine / slide steel down spines / I watch heat / steam off my skin when Westerners drop / *I love you's* / into conversation / like blueberries / hitting soft muffin dough / I convert it to shillings / wince

December 2000 / one hundred twenty shillings to the British pound / ninety Kenyan shillings to the US dollar

My sister Sneha and I wait for our parents / at San Francisco's international airport

Four hours / after their plane landed / they have not
emerged / and we know / with the hopeless rage of third-
world citizens / of African passport holders / that the
sum of their lives and labour / dreams and sacrifice / is
being measured / sifted / weighed / found wanting / by
Immigration

Somewhere deep in the airport's underbelly / in a room
rank with fear and despair / my parents / who have
travelled 27 hours / across three continents / to see their
children / are being interrogated by immigration officers

My father / the footsoldier / numb with exhaustion / is
tossing away three decades of struggle / with reckless
resolve / telling them / *take the passports / take them /
stamp them / no readmission / ever / just let me out to see my
daughters*

My mother / the general / dizzy / with desperation / cuts
him off / shouts him down / demands / *listen to me / I'm
the one / who filled in the visa forms*

In her mind / her lip curls / she thinks / *these Americans /
call themselves / so advanced so / modern but still / in the
year 2000 / they think it must be the husband in charge / they
won't let the wife speak*

On her face / a lifetime of / battle-honed skill and charm
turns like a heat lamp / onto the Immigration man who
yawns / stretches / relents / it's late / he's tired /
wants his dinner / and my parents / trained from birth to
extend Kenyan hospitality / open their bags and offer /
their sandwiches / to this man who would have sent
them back / without a second thought

In the darkened lobby | Sneha and I watch the empty exit |
our whole American | dream bought with | their lives |
hisses mockery | around our rigid bodies | we swallow
sobs | because they raised us to be tough | they raised us
to be fighters | and into that clenched haze of | not crying |
here they come | hunched over their luggage carts | our
tiny | fierce | fragile | dogged | indomitable parents

Hugged tight | they stink | of thirty-one hours in transit |
hugged tighter | we all stink | with the bravado | of all the
years | pain bitten down | on gargantuan hopes | holding on |
through near-disasters | never ever | giving in to | softness

The stench rises off us | unbearable | of what was
never said

something is | bursting the walls | of my arteries |
something is | pounding its way | up my throat | volcano
rising | finally I understand | why I'm a poet

15. MANGAL SUTRA
[Mother's Voice]

Dearest Shailja,

Yes, I know, a mangal sutra necklace is normally given to a woman by her husband. However, both your sisters, Shruti and Sneha, each have a mangal sutra now. You know we have always treated all three of you equally. Since you have stubbornly refused to get married, it seems your mangal sutra has to come from your mother instead of your husband!

But this does not absolve you of your duty to settle down in life! If you want me to find a man for you, I shall, with the greatest of pleasure. You know we have been turning down proposals for you since you were thirteen.

You have been brainwashed by the mass media, who concentrate on the tragedies of life: flood, fire, famine, fighting. But in the midst of all this is youth, with its dreams of happiness. Why not concentrate on the beauty and miracle of life, instead of on suffering and pain?

Married life has its ups and downs, but ultimately, it is also great fun. After forty years of married life together, and all our labours and worries, your father and I have finally found the time to relax and enjoy leisure. Even though your father is turning into a grumpy, senile old man, neither of us would want to be alone at our age. Besides, women age much more gracefully than men. This is just a fact of life that one must put up with.

You know that mangal sutra literally means: "thread of good will." The two strands of black beads are protection against evil. The one I have given you is very modern and fashionable, but in a traditional mangal sutra, there are three granthis – three knots of commitment. The first knot stands for intention. The second knot is for the declaration that takes place in the marriage ceremony. The third knot is for the lifelong performance of the commitment you make.

So there you go, dearest daughter. You have had your years of sexual experimentation and adventures. You have fully enjoyed your travels and feminism and independence. Now find a wonderful man to marry and make a home with. Life is but a prize for winning LOVE. Time and Tide do not wait for anyone, and you are getting on in age!

Today is a very cold day. There was so much mist in the early morning air. For some reason, I keep remembering our visit to San Francisco one year ago! All the beautiful walks and picnics and the trip to the wine country, and I felt so proud of you; like all my friends say, each of my daughters is two sons put together!

We love you very much, despite all your tantrums and fault finding with us.

Bye.
Mummy

16. BORN TO A LAW

Trousseau.
The wealth a woman takes
when she leaves the home of her parents.
Etymology: Old French.
From trousse –
bundle – and trousser –
to tie up.

Mother.
I will never live
the cocoon of safety
you dreamed of for your daughters.

Do you see? I will always be called
to stride across danger zones,
to shout forbidden words to other fugitives.

But Mummy, look.
I am forging a ship of glittering songs
to sail your jewels in,
staking a masthead of verbs
from which to fly your saris!

This work that filigrees and inlays
all your legacies,
that snakes across borders,
dodges visa controls,
this
is my intention.
Declaration.
Lifelong execution.

The wealth this woman took
when she left the home of her parents.
The deep, hard,
complex beauty
that unfurls
when saris speak.

Because, Mummy,
you of all people
know
how we were born to a law
that states

before we claim a word,
we steep it
in terror and shit,
in hope and joy and grief,
in labour, endurance,
vision costed out
in decades of our lives.

We have to sweat and curse it,
pray and keen it,
crawl and bleed it

With the very marrow
of our bones
we have to earn
its meaning.

NOTES

IDI AMIN
— "Secret documents declassified...": *Times of Zambia*, October 13, 2005.

MAU MAU
— Oral testimonies of camp survivors adapted from: *Imperial Reckoning: The Untold Story of Britain's Gulag in Kenya*, by Caroline Elkins (Henry Holt and Company, 2005). Used with permission of the author.
    — 1956 *Sunday Post* interview and quote from Katherine Warren-Gash: Ibid.
    — Jomo Kenyatta's speech, 1964: Ibid
— "[F]ewer than 100 whites and over 25,000 Africans died...": John Blacker. 2007. "The demography of Mau Mau: fertility and mortality in Kenya in the 1950s: a demographer's viewpoint," *African Affairs* 106, Number 423: 205-227.

SWORE I'D NEVER WEAR CLOTHES I COULDN'T RUN OR FIGHT IN
— "That is a well-governed state...": Santi Parva, epilogue to Mahabharata. Cited by Carol Lee Flinders, *At The Root of This Longing*, (HarperSanFrancisco, 1999).

MIGRANT SONG
—"Israeli soldiers shot and killed a 9-year old girl...": *Daily Telegraph* (UK), January 27th, 2006,
—"Metallica's James Hetfield...": Quote from interview on Fresh Air, NPR, reproduced in *The Nation*, December 26, 2005.

THE SKY HAS NOT CHANGED COLOUR
— "Adrian Blomfield reports...": "Prostitutes 'told to fake rape claims,'" *Daily Telegraph* (UK), October 2, 2003.

WHAT CAME OUT OF THE SUITCASE

Observations harvested from sari-viewing by eight friends and director Kim Cook, blended with my own associations and responses.

SARIS

RED GEORGETTE, PLAIN (MAU MAU)
Matches the suitcase. Everything is red through its diaphanous screen. In India, at Diwali, upper middle-class people give bright synthetic saris to servants because they wash easily. It's stamped: *Surat Mills, American Georgette*. But near the border, a smaller stamp: *Made in China*. Looks demure, but becomes transparent when wet.

GREEN / MAGENTA DHOOP CHAYYA (DOUBLE-WEAVE) SILK
Two tones, red and earthy green, shot through with zari. The two colors flow into each other, giving it depth and density. Chiaroscuro, light and shade. Ganga / Jamuna: the confluence of two mighty rivers, the cradle of Indo-Muslim civilization. This is a sari to run a corporation in. South Indian conservative. But look: a touch of subversion – a frayed border intentionally woven into the pattern. In the US, this would show poverty – in India, it's the privilege of fragile finery. No bouties (embroidery / attachments).

PINK HEAVY SILK WITH GREEN BORDER
An Easter Princess sari. The threads at the back are neat – very fragile. If you cut a thread, the whole sari could unravel. It's the exact same colors as the Sex Pistols album *Never Mind The Bollocks*. Makes my mouth water for special bharfee – the milk-solid fudge that is normally white, but for special days (weddings and festivals) is mixed with lurid food coloring by the mithaiwallahs to become pink and green.

BRIGHT GREEN GEORGETTE WITH BLACK AND
GOLD EMBROIDERED FLOWERS

This sari is pure Sixties, making me think of women with bobs and
black eyeliner. An arts and crafts sari – hand-embroidered with
glitter. Both sensual and sexual, it reveals and hides. The fabric
moves, evoking classic Bollywood scenes – wet saris, saris caught
on trees, saris fluttering in the breeze. The velvet flowers on its
borders are like bindis of soft felt with gold centers. Green is a
Muslim color. Or the taste of pistachio kulfi.

ORANGE / OCHRE HEAVY SILK

This sari was made in Mysore, famous for its silks. Mysore silks
are supposed to have a unique sheen, scent, and drape. It's a power
color – sober, weighty, serious. The color of sandalwood and
saffron. Mirabai, mystic poet, sang of bhagava, or ochre – the color
of renunciation, of total surrender to being dissolved and remolded
into a new form. Her hymn to Krishna – *whatever guise you want me
to adopt, I will* – could be a migrant manifesto: assimilation as the
price of refuge. The pattern on the sari looks like fleur de lys or the
Venus of Willendorf. The # 47 stamped on the corner always makes
me think of 1947 – India's independence.

ORANGE GEORGETTE WITH WHITE / PURPLE
EMBROIDERED FLOWERS

In the US, this sari looks psychedelic because of its color
combination – purple and orange. But it reminds me of how bold
and playful my mother is. The flowers, which look almost like four-
leaf clovers, are loops of cord stitched onto the sari, representing
hours of hand embroidery. Satin stitch is used for the purple
centers. My mother loves embroidery; she still keeps a sampler of
embroidery stitches that she made as a schoolgirl. "Isn't it pretty?"
she'd ask, tracing the stitches. A Jalebi. Carrot halwa. Kollum –
white rice powder used to make intricate geometric patterns in
the South of India. Five million Tamil women all over the world,
in slum hovels and in mansions, begin the day by making kollum

patterns on their thresholds for the protection and blessing of their family.

CHOCOLATE / SILVER SILK

A sari that transforms my body into an altar, worthy of being worshipped. It makes me feel like a priestess – holy and regal. The deep brown color enfolds me in liquid mahogany, with ivory inlay. The richness of the fabric magically appears effervescent and light, even as its drape suggests an elegant weightiness.

GREEN PRINT ON WHITE SILK

I think of this as a Navaratri sari, but the images are all of Holi games, a spring festival where men and women spray each other with colored dyes. Phallic patterns grace the fabric – a man's flute points suggestively at a woman's dancing body. The men on the sari wear Mughal turbans and curly-topped sarimshai shoes from Morocco. They carry flutes and drums. I have a photo of my mother wearing this sari, her eyes laughing, her hair long, wavy, falling down her back. I love the lightness of the silk, the susurrations of it when I walk. The way it moulds to my body.

PALE GREEN AND PINK HEAVY SILK WITH FRINGED PALLAV

The sari's colors evoke the light-dappled sea at sunrise. The ends flutter like mini-ripples on a beach. Old fashioned. Hand-tied tassels at the end of the fringed pallav – a way of finishing off so the threads don't unravel. The colors, soft and muted, are vegetable dyes, not chemicals. The weavers who did this kind of work were untouchables. Why does that make it so precious? One of the epic novels I imagined as a child was of a family of poor weavers in Banarasi who spent their lives creating magnificent saris they could never wear themselves.

MAGENTA SILK CHIFFON WITH BLACK PRINT

Colors are powerful goddesses. I associate this sari with Draupadi, strong and beautiful. The silver border is formal. The magenta, rich yet airy, is called "rani" in Gujarati. My parents call it "falsa," which is a sour fruit from Pakistan that tastes a little like pomegranate and dyes your mouth pink. A taste that indelibly colored my childhood. The chiffon is the lightest of all in the saris in the suitcase – ephemeral, gossamer, playful and seductive. Precisely because of that, wearing this feels like a responsibility. In it, I'm a walking flirtation, inviting exotification. I have seen Indian tourists at the Golden Gate Bridge in exquisite saris like this one, worn with sneakers and puffy jackets.

PINK FAUX CREPE DE CHINE WITH RAFFIA WORK
(THE MOTHER SARI)

The color of cotton candy, with the feel of a little girl's nightie. The girliest sari in the suitcase. It is in the Parsi (Zoroastrian) style – simple, no pattern, applied borders. Japanese fan shapes are woven in the raffia work, border, and pallav. With its very modest long-sleeved blouse, it feels like a 1950s sari. But in fact it was my training sari – the one my sister and I used as teenagers. Learning to wear a sari is a rite of passage. What were other Kenyan girls doing while I was learning how to wear a sari? Practicing Michael Jackson's *Thriller* moves? Collecting Lionel Ritchie cassettes? Dancing at Bubbles and Carnivore, the trendy nightspots for Nairobi's wealthy teens? If you got too close to heat, this sari would melt. A real risk during Diwali – women in saris catch fire from lamps and became living pyres. Dowry deaths – kitchen deaths – women whose saris were set alight or caught fire. Danger embedded in the most innocent and modest of saris.

TURQUOISE SILK DHOOP CHAYYA
(DOUBLE WEAVE, PEACOCK EFFECT OF SHIFTING COLOURS)

A friend told me a story of a man who took LSD and saw the shimmering lights of the Aurora Borealis. It triggered a memory of his mother's sari hemline. A magical iridescence offering warmth and comfort in the cold of night. This two-tone sari is my Aurora Borealis.

SAND-COLORED HEAVY SILK
My friends saw this as the ugly stepchild of the bunch – a rusty
'70s Buick. But I felt really protective of it when the others didn't
like it – it's one of my favorites! Closest to my skin color, the one I
can best imagine growing naturally out of my body. I like to wrap
myself in it without blouse or petticoat, to revel in the silk against
bare skin.

MAGENTA CHIFFON WITH HEAVY GOLD EMBROIDERY
In every context, this sari exudes strength and delicacy – the
transcendent power of love. American georgette, made in India.
The embroidery, a celestial gold, evokes Oshun, who represents
love, wealth, and creativity. Even the motif – of peacocks – recalls
Oshun's animal. Was Yeats envisioning this sari in "Aesh Wishes for
the Cloths of Heaven"?

> Had I the heavens' embroidered cloths,
> Enwrought with golden and silver light,
> The blue and the dim and the dark cloths
> Of night and light and the half light,
> I would spread the cloths under your feet:
> But I, being poor, have only my dreams;
> I have spread my dreams under your feet;
> Tread softly because you tread on my dreams.

This would be garish anywhere other than a wedding. I thought it
was a garchoru – a wedding sari – but Mum told me it wasn't, just
a very elaborate sari to be worn at a family wedding. It's so heavy
that my neck droops when I drape it over my head. Magenta – falsa,
rani - a rare color in the US. Represents depth, dignity, royalty,
vibrancy, celebration, and uncertainty (red or blue?). Fuchsia
flowers are also used in love spells for Oshun. Perhaps it's the color
of my mother's broken heart: the weight and magnificence – the
splendor – of her sacrifices.

GAGRA CHOLIS: DECORATED BLOUSE + SKIRT + CHUNDARI (HALF-SARI)

BLUE GAGRA CHOLI WITH MAGENTA CHUNDARI
Gagra cholis are for Navaratri dances – the annual nine-day celebration of the harvest and the goddess. I didn't learn until adulthood that they're specific to Gujarat. Women from other parts of India see them as a folk costume. The chundari over the blue looks purple. It's made from French chiffon – very light. The pallav must have come from a sari, it's so wide.

GREEN WITH GOLD EMBROIDERY
This looks Ethiopian / Eritrean. The vibrant green marks it as a gagra choli for a young girl. It evokes puberty, springtime, fertility. Elephant and peacock motifs. Eastern European. Peasant. Bedouin. Migration. Carnival. Circus. Bordello. The Castro. Its embroidery is in the salma-sitara style: salma is chainstitch braiding, sitara is sequins. In Pakistan, no images are allowed on saris or gagra cholis, because the Quran forbids images.

YELLOW AND RED BHANDNI – MIRRORWORK
Gujarati style. Ribbon borders with fake bhandni (tie-and-dye) print, in the colours of the ANC and Rastafarians. Mirrors on the skirt look back at you. A goddess symbol – an inverted triangle directly beneath the navel. Curves at the bottom evoke minarets – Mughal. Bells are attention grabbing. Reminiscent of Superwoman or Almodovar – the bold, in-your-face colours, the triangular shapes, the reflecting mirrors and multiple possible meanings. This is the gagra choli I wear in what became the iconic *Migritude* photo – I'm crossing a bridge, carrying the red suitcase, looking back over my shoulder.

II.

Shadow
Book

Aap mua vina swarge na javay.
You cannot go to heaven without dying first.

— GUJARATI PROVERB

Theatre is not a finished product; it happens on its legs.
– *Kim Cook, Director of* Migritude

Any piece of writing is necessarily the gestalt of a sea of ideas, influences, and encounters. This Shadow Book *is a collection of shells and seaweed from the shoreline. It makes no attempt to be a comprehensive narrative of the making of* Migritude*. It's more like an extended debrief with an old friend: behind-the-scenes and after-the-fact vignettes, memories, and associations. The idea is to illuminate* Migritude *by offering context – both the underside and the offshoots of the stories.*

PRELUDE: HOW AMBI BECAME PAISLEY

I'd never given the shape a second thought. But when I invited friends to look at my trousseau and tell me what they saw, Huma mentioned in passing that the word "paisley" came from the village in Scotland to which the British abducted India's textile trade. That launched my investigation.

I found that ambi didn't even originate in India, but went all the way back to Babylon. I was crestfallen. I'd wanted the story to be a one-way, straightforward colonial appropriation. Instead, I had to engage with multiple migrations, roll back several more eras of history.

There's a large framed poster of a cave painting from Sri Lanka on my parents' dining room wall in Nairobi. It depicts the Goddess, in stone, earth, and sepia tones. *Astarte, shameless goddess of the fecund feminine.* She holds a three-petalled flower. Her body is lush, with large descending breasts and three rolls of belly fat.

My mother always told me it was "my" picture – a gift from a Sri Lankan friend when I was a baby. He said it represented my name: the carvings and paintings of the goddess in the mountain caves are called *shailaja* or *of the mountain*. The Sanskrit word *shail* – mountain stone – is the root of the English *shale*.

Parijat's feet open the performance of *Migritude*. When

the show begins, I'm lying on the stage. I can feel the vibrations – the force and precision of her footwork – under my body. The feet of the goddess, drumming the world into being.

A fellow artist, Robert Karimi, called it *the rhythm that set our heartbeats for the rest of the show.*

> *Da-DAH-da-da-da-DAH-da-da-da-DAH!*
> *Four beats of the ankle bells. Clink. Clink. Clink. Clink.*
> *Da-DAH-da-da-da-DAH-da-da-da-DAH!*

The end of the footbeats is my cue to open my eyes and begin.

PART I: NAIROBI, KENYA (1972 – 1989)

I grew up in Kenya during the Moi years. When those who spoke out were routinely arrested, detained without trial, beaten, tortured, exiled, killed. We read daily news stories about journalists, activists, even students, who were jailed for sedition. Every so often, our literature teacher would tell us that such-and-such a poet had been banned – and we'd dutifully cross out their name and poems out in our school textbooks.

How do I know when a piece of writing wants to leap from print into performance? When I itch to see it embodied, hear it aloud. When it pushes me up against the limitations of language on the page, so the next revision has to be worked out in voice and movement. I walk a lot of my writing, the way you walk a dog – it completes itself in motion.

1. IDI AMIN

Idi Amin was the villain of my childhood. When he was overthrown, Kenya's newspapers ran gory stories of the human heads found in his fridge and the sadistic games he played with prisoners – forcing them to have sex in front of him, to ransom their lives with their "performance."

What I didn't know was that Idi Amin was a guard in the King's African Rifles, the Native troops used to quell the Mau Mau uprising in Kenya. He learned to torture and terrorize from the finest – the British army.

I knew from childhood that one of the epics I would write when I grew up and became an author was the tale of Asians being thrown out of Uganda.

My mother was the one who told that story. How she and my father, along with all the other Asians in Nairobi, went to the railway station carrying food, milk, water, and clothing for Asians on the trains coming out of Uganda. She was the one who saw the man on the platform, holding his child, crying.

That image, of a grown man crying, seared itself on my imagination. Crying while he held a child – which meant he was a Daddy – but Daddies don't cry! Can Daddies really cry? Wouldn't that split the foundations of the world?

In the show, when I reveal that Britain, Israel, and the

US sponsored Amin's coup, I'm unwrapping the sari I put on at the start of the piece. I gather it in folds as it comes off my body. Shake the folds together with a snap. Hang the sari firmly on a bar as I say, "A man we can do business with."

2. THE JEWELLERY
[Mother's Voice]

The terrors of telling a story. I don't know enough. I'll get it wrong. I don't have enough time or skill or talent to do it justice. It's not mine to tell. I'll be attacked, criticized, ignored, laughed at. If no one else has done it yet, what makes me think I can?

I imagined that everyone must have childhood memories of watching their mother dress up. That transformation from an ordinary, often-harassed woman into an empress. Not true, it turns out. But watching my mother get dressed for a special event, usually a wedding, was our childhood theatre. She'd stand in front of the full-length mirror inside the door of her wardrobe as my sisters and I sat on my parents' double bed and watched her.

She let us take turns choosing which sari she should wear. I always picked the golden one I thought transformed her into a queen. Unlike many other women, who whipped saris around themselves daily, my mother wore trousers in her daily life – a mark of her modernity. When she put on a sari, it was ritual, ceremony. She brought a precise choreography to the folding of pleats at the waist, the extension of her arm to measure the length of the pallav. We imitated her finger movements, pleating our "play sari", a child-sized length of sari fabric, with our small, untrained hands.

To this day, I have not seen another woman wear a sari as well as my mother does, match her regal grace. She told us her siblings used to tease her for practising posture as a girl, mocked her pride when she held her shoulders back.

I spent hours experimenting with different wrapping styles for the performance. I explored using a sari to convey combat, or digging a field, or construction labor. I learned insider tricks, like a hidden knot at the waistband to hold the sari up.

Once we visited a friend of my mother's and found her casually putting her sari on over her petticoat, the door open to her house servant in the next room. My mother's eyes widened. She couldn't get over the vulgarity.

3. HISTORY LESSON

The crimson sari shaped the choreography of this piece. Told me it wanted to be knotted for the oral testimonies of the women in the camps. Each knot a dead child. When I lay the knotted sari in a circle, then gather it up in my arms, it feels like a part of my own body. I hang it on the bar on the stage: a glowing rope of knots, a testament to children killed by Empire.

In one of her poems, *Further Notes to Clark*, Lucille Clifton asks: *What have you ever travelled toward / more than your own safety?*

At Mount Kenya Safari Club, they have a traditional dance show every evening. The dancers, in full "tribal" regalia – lion-mane headdresses, spears, grass skirts – troop onto the lawn outside the lounge. Separated from the dancers by a glass wall, the tourists sit on easy chairs inside, big wood fires roaring. Watch the natives drum and dance outside, under spotlights. When the dance is over, the dancers wave goodbye and vanish into the night.

4. SWORE I'D NEVER WEAR CLOTHES I COULDN'T RUN OR FIGHT IN

Sometimes beauty is so profoundly subjective that just sharing the beauty that we know of each other becomes profoundly political.
— Patrick "Pato" Herbert, San Francisco-based visual artist

I want to enlarge my audiences' concepts of what is desirable. To make rage beautiful and grief compelling. To keep expanding the definitions of beauty.

I needed to learn how to own my body on stage, without disowning my voice. How to be potent, sensual, alive, in performance – warrior, goddess, child, athlete – with no conflict or tension between all these different selves. How to link these selves with the telling of truths.

I had so much fun with *Don't stride, Shailja!* Where I stomp around the stage kicking my way out of a sari that's hobbling my knees.

5. I NEVER WANTED DAUGHTERS
[Mother's Voice]

My mother insists that this is not true. It is the only part of the script she disagrees with. She says we were always wanted. That when she sighed, *If only you had a brother*, or suggested that we had to make up for not being boys, it was her fear talking. That a mother's love in a time of danger can look and feel like rage, like rejection.

I tell her it's OK to own up to ambivalence. To have felt everything – love and rage towards her daughters, alongside a longing for sons.

The sari I wear in this piece would melt if it got too close to heat. Evoking the horror stories of women whose saris caught fire from open flame lamps and aarti trays at Diwali: they became living pyres.

This was our training sari – the one my mother used to teach us how to put on a sari when we were teenagers.

6. SHILLING LOVE PART I

The English compositions we wrote in primary and secondary school were peopled by white characters with English names. We set them in European or US cities and schools and inserted ourselves into those landscapes. Or we stole freely from US sitcoms and soaps – *Good Times*, *Dallas*. One of my classmates, in an essay on "The Dangers of Hitchhiking," reproduced, blow by blow, an episode of *Diff'rent Strokes* that had run the previous night on Kenyan TV. Didn't even change the names of the characters – just cast herself in the starring role. The English teacher commented, *You should use your own ideas in future!* And gave her a mark of 75%.

In all those years, there was only one teacher who ever challenged this erasure of our own lives. Ironically, he was a British expatriate. He asked my Standard Seven class why we used English names and places in our compositions instead of Kenyan ones. We stared at him, confused: a classroom of 11 year olds, who had never imagined that our reality had any place in literature. Finally, one girl raised her hand: *That's what is in the books we read.*

Shilling Love germinated on a hike with a man I was dating. As we walked the Skyline-to-the-Sea trail in the Santa Cruz mountains, I described my childhood to him – the anxiety of the '80s and '90s in Kenya, my parents' sacrifices, my drive to succeed, to repay them, to make it all worthwhile.

He said: *God your childhood sounds terrible! All struggle and duty!*

I was shocked. I thought I had been showing him how much my parents loved me.

Theatre is relationship. A body in front of other bodies.
Unfiltered, unedited, unmanipulated. In real time. If I
screw up on stage, everyone participates in the moment.
What then, is writing?

I got Saved when I was 10 years old. My best friend,
Nina, was the English-Dutch daughter of Christian
missionaries. She made me read Revelations 13 – the fate
in store for me and my family and community. But if I
accepted Jesus as my personal Saviour, if I gave my life
to Him, His death would erase my sins. Then I could save
my family, too.

For every soul she brought to Jesus, Nina got a star
in her crown in heaven. She wasn't sure if I had a crown
in heaven too. She thought you might have to earn a
crown by a certain number of years of being saved.

I went to Bible Club every week. Thursday
lunchtimes. Learned bible verse and bible stories. Sang
an adaptation of Woody Guthrie: *This land for Jee-zus / He
is the answer / This land for Jee-zus / He died to save us!* to Mr.
Gitonga's guitar. Christians and guitars went together.

When I stayed the weekend at Nina's house, I
tentatively hazarded the tenet of my Hindu upbringing:
maybe all religions were different paths to the same god?
Her mother countered quickly with: *But we offer heaven
and salvation!*

When my mother found out I was "a Christian," she
asked: Had they given me anything to drink? Blindfolded
me? Fed me anything? I was forbidden to attend Bible
Club, or to be friends with Nina anymore.

This made me a hero to the missionary community – a child who was being persecuted by her heathen parents for coming to Jesus. One of the missionaries, a young American woman, wrote in my autograph book: *You have been such an inspiration to me this year! I can tell you truly love Jesus as your Saviour.*

7. THE MAKING (MIGRANT SONG)

Performing is so much easier than writing because it's collaborative. Faced with an audience, there's no option but to show up and offer all that I can. Writing is singular and isolating, and I'm not a self-starter. People ask all the time about the process of taking work from the page to the stage. In my experience, the real challenge is the reverse journey: from the interactive co-creation of the stage to the loneliness of cranking it out on the page.

The choreography for *Migritude* was developed in New York with Parijat. Working with her, I caught a tiny glimpse of the vocabulary of dance. How the distance of arm from torso, the amount of energy in a leg, are physical text that the audience reads without even knowing that they're reading it.

I call my parents in Nairobi, tell my father how nervous I am about the first work-in-progress showing of *Migritude*, which is a week away.

He says: *Why? You're a seasoned performer by now.*

I say: *I'm doing things for this show that I haven't done before. Acting. Moving on stage. Working with lights and costumes and props. I'm scared that I'm not very good at it yet, and people will see that, and be disappointed.*

He says: *Why do you judge yourself? Let others judge you; that's their business. You just do what you've set out to do.*

8. UNDER AND OVER

Halfway through the writing of *Migritude*, I have the most vivid dream of my life:

I am with my sister Shruti on the Ngong Hills escarpment in Kenya, overlooking the Great Rift Valley. As children, we made regular family excursions to the viewing point to watch the full moon rise over the Rift.

The moon has risen, and we have a journey before us. I am impatient to leave, but Shruti says, *It's not time yet.* I watch a gauzy cloud swirl around the moon like a chiffon scarf and think, *We're going to be late!*

I look at Shruti. The wind streams through her hair, blows it straight back behind her. Her face in the moonlight is so radiant and certain that my irritation dissolves.

Suddenly, flames shoot out of the moon. They leap through the cloud scarf, devouring it, until the whole moon is exposed and blazing with fire, but somehow still cool and luminous. I laugh out loud at the wonder of it and cry, *Shruti, look! The moon's on fire!*

That means it's time, she says. *Now we can go.*

9. AUSTRALIA
[Mother's Voice]

Why do you live in the US when you're so critical of it?
Because I'd rather be in the country that's dropping the bombs
than in the country the bombs are falling on. Wouldn't you?

I got my green card in New Orleans. City of big dreamers.
Start of my American odyssey. All my possessions fit
in my backpack. No fixed address, no fixed destination.
First stop: post office, to collect mail. First envelope:
my green card. Forwarded by my uncle in Columbus,
Ohio, which had been my landing airport, my official
"Port of Entry" into the United States. Second envelope:
a check. Ten dollars. For a poem I'd send to a tiny journal
in Columbus, the *Short North Gazette*. I knew it was a sign
from the gods: in a land where I was finally legal, I could
be paid – for a poem.

10. THE SKY HAS NOT CHANGED
COLOR

The first time I rehearsed this with Kim, my instinct
was to turn my back to the audience while speaking of
violation. Kim suggested that I sit on the stage and push
myself back with my hands. That evolved into the final
choreography, where Parijat and I enter lying flat on our
backs, pushing ourselves across the stage with our feet
while pulling a length of black cloth with us. The black
cloth becomes a river, a demarcation of space and time.
Hours of repeating, rehearsing, adjusting were required
to perfect the direction and pace for that one-minute
entrance. The fabric had to be folded just so at the start
in order to unfold evenly into a long line.

At the line *They are the noble savages*, I pull pages of
Maasai images out of a tourist photo book and hand
them to the front row of the audience.

At *May the redness overtake them*, I pick up the river cloth
and begin to loop it around my elbow and shoulder. Pull the
energy tighter and tighter, bind the curse into its vortex.

11. MAASAI WOMEN RIOTING
[Mother's Voice]

The stories I wrote as a child were imitations of the
Enid Blyton books I read. I invented English boarding
schools, along with uniforms and supplies lists for
the girls who went to them, right down to underwear.
Creating these ordered worlds of material security was
incredibly satisfying.

During the years the rapes were happening, I
was reading Kipling and Georgette Heyer in school.
Entranced by fantasy worlds of British schoolboys and
Regency romance.

We saw the British soldiers in Nanyuki sometimes.
They came in from their military bases for drinks at the
national park lodges. Always large, faces sunburned
raw pink or angry red, looking sweaty and miserably
uncomfortable in their thick khaki uniforms. Belted and
booted in the heat.

12. DREAMING IN GUJARATI

My voice coach says the voice needs to be moved and caressed like bread dough. *Knead it. Move the pitches, the resonance. Tap into lower pitches, but don't hold there. Keep your voice flexible, silky. Watch the glottal stops. When excited, don't lose your sense of space and depth. The larger you get, the deeper you need to get, the more space you need behind you. Zap meaning rather than force at the audience. Let them come to you. Don't pull your voice out from above. Rest in the throne of yourself. Think skeletal alignment. Float the spine up. Don't clench the abdomen; relax and re-engage. Relax and re-engage.*

When Shruti left Kenya to study in the UK, my father sat himself down once a week, sweated and struggled to fill an aerogramme to her. When done, he asked me or Sneha to read it and correct spelling mistakes, grammatical errors in the English.

The novelist May Sarton has a line in one of her books: *Perhaps, in the end, this is why one is a poet. So that once in a lifetime, one can say the right words to the right person.*

13. DAD'S VISA
[Mother's Voice]

My father refuses to travel any more to the US. Post 9/11, he
gets racially profiled. Every time. At Heathrow, I watched
the security make a Sikh man strip, right down to his
underwear. Remove his turban to reveal his knot of hair.

It's early morning in Nairobi. I'm leaving the house for
a foundation-sponsored seminar. My father asks, semi-
derisively: *What are you talking about today?* He has little
respect for the notion that talking is work.

   I say: *We're discussing masculinities, Dad. Yesterday,
it was just Kenyans, but today, some American scholars are
joining us.*

   My father grabs a piece of ginger, places it precisely in
the centre of the chopping board, and hacks it swiftly into
small chunks. *You tell those Americans that a six-foot Marine
can be made to lick his own spittle by a four-foot Gurkha!*

14. SHILLING LOVE II

When I perform the first part of this piece, I become the
watcher. I have to see my parents and the immigration

official so vividly that the audience sees them too. Until they come towards us: *my tiny / fierce / fragile / dogged / indomitable parents*.

Then I step into the piece again.

I did a performance of *Migritude* at a bookshop in Genoa, Italy. Wondered how much of it could possibly resonate with an urban Italian audience. The bookshop owner said afterwards that he grew up in Calabria, a poor rural region of Italy. Conditions there were so harsh that people would often say, *Kiss your children only while they're sleeping*. Meaning, any affection shown while they were awake would weaken them in their battle for survival.

At *Something is bursting the walls of my arteries*, energy surges through my body. Like a rocket ignited, I am propelled into motion. At the San Francisco premiere, where the stage was large enough, I got to run around the stage at this line. I recall of the brush of silk from the hanging saris across my face and arms as I spun. Every cell charged with joy.

15. MANGAL SUTRA
[Mother's Voice]

As a teenage feminist, I put mangal sutras in the same category as wedding rings: a symbol of bondage, something that branded a woman as chattel. Moveable property.

When my mother gave me one, I was stunned. It meant: *Your chosen path is no less serious, no less worthy of ceremonial recognition, than your sisters' marriages.*

I couldn't have imagined breaking the rule that mangal sutras were only for married women. That they could only be given to a woman by her husband. In this act, my mother showed me up as the traditionalist. Appointed herself the revolutionary.

Her gift showed me that the three granthis of the mangal sutra could be a blueprint for a creative life. An activist life. *My* life. Intention. Declaration. Execution.

16. BORN TO A LAW

The last line of the show was its starting point.

Migritude began as a quest to use my trousseau in my work. A vision for a masthead of verbs to fly my saris from.

6am in Nairobi means sunrise. Trees erupt into bird chatter. Early in the morning, Nairobi smells of rain and smoke. Later in the day, exhaust fumes take over. Seventeen years after I left for the UK – *learn and study, succeed, learn and study, succeed* – I have brought my work home.

My parents feed me as if I'd just come off a month-long fast. Luscious mangoes, which my father has carefully ripened for me. Thick, buttery avocadoes. Hot chapatis, straight from the clay griddle, gleaming with butter. Shiro studded with raisins and almonds, shiny with ghee. Chunky dhal fragrant with fresh chillies and ginger.

Mealtimes are a comical dance of both of them leaping up every few minutes to bring me something else – herbal salt, pickles, yoghurt – heaping more onto my plate, urging me to *eat, eat, eat.*

Journalists often tell me they've never heard an Asian voice the radical politics they hear in my work. I am asked repeatedly for my thoughts on "Indians in Kenya." I say: *I don't really have any knowledge about Indians in Kenya. But I have a lot to say about brown Kenyans.*

I point out that just as black Kenyans who challenged single-party rule and the betrayal of Kenya's independence were exiled, imprisoned, or killed, so also were dissenting brown Kenyans silenced – through assassination, deportation, stripping of citizenship.

When Youssou N'Dour sang at Nairobi's legendary Carnivore restaurant in 2005, he drew a capacity crowd of 4,500. *Migritude*'s premiere performance in Kenya draws slightly less. A lot less, in fact. Only 59 tickets sold (we'd projected 200). Most glaring, and personally disappointing, is the absence of my own brown Kenyan community, aside from a few progressive activists, journalists, and friends.

But the press is there in force. KTN, the national TV network, films the entire show. Journalists from Kenya's two national dailies bombard me with questions after the performance. Features on me and *Migritude* run in the papers every day for the next six days – including a cover story in the weekend magazine of *The Nation,* the highest-circulation national newspaper. The title is *Seeking Justice Through Poetry*.

And the response to *Migritude* from the 59 people there is nothing short of electric. They surround me on stage afterward, almost overwhelm me with eagerness, appreciation, thoughts, questions. I am amazed at how my work has sliced through ethnic and socio-economic boundaries. Some of the most enthusiastic responses and persistent questions come from a group of MCs and b-boys who, I am later told, were all street children until a few years ago. One of them tells me how powerfully affected he was by the integration of history, politics, and economics into my poetry. He asks: *What obstacles will I face in writing like this?*

Someone else, a brown Kenyan, tells me he was moved to tears by "Shilling Love." He was embarrassed by his emotion, until he looked around and saw another listener, a black Kenyan, also crying. *I have never had this experience before.*

In the finale of the show, the audience has finally earned the right to see the saris in all their splendour. Because they've engaged with the violence and violation beneath. Sat through the unbearable and absorbed it. Listened to voices of women from within the bootprint of Empire. They've paid for the experience of beauty, sensuality – and they understand the cost.

I open the suitcase fully, shake out a twin set of khangas from Zanzibar – black and white, with ambi patterns – and spread them on the floor. Unpack the saris onto them, one by one. Show off the borders and embroidery. I toss the bright green georgette in the air – one of my favourite moments in the show. Trace the silver zari on the heavy chocolate silk. Hold the softest sandalwood Mysore silk to my face and inhale. Wrap the turquoise blue around me. The last one I bring out is the wedding sari, described by a friend as *the day the earth stood still* – magenta chiffon, stiff and glittering with heavy peacock motif embroidery.

The question asked of those who return, voiced or implicit, is always: *What have you brought? What do you have to show for your years abroad?* You're expected to display wealth. Achievement, accomplishment, accumulation. And to come laden with gifts: German cars, iPods, and designer handbags are all good.

   I brought *Migritude*. A tapestry of poetry, history, politics, packed into a suitcase, embedded in my body, rolled out into theatre. An accounting of Empire enacted on the bodies of women.

   I grew up a brown minority citizen of a post-independence black African nation. Everything citizens of the global North take for granted as rights, down to expressions of love from parents to children, have been for me painfully won privileges to be cherished and defended.

On Kenya Airways flights, *Local Time At Destination* is rendered in Kiswahili as *Saa Ya Kinyumbani Ya Mwisho Wa Safari.*

   Literal translation: *Time of the home at the end of the journey.*

III.

THE MAKING
and Other Poems

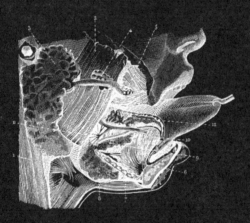

Mounam sammati lakshanam.
Silence implies consent / acceptance.

— SANSKRIT PROVERB

The impulse to create begins – often terribly and fearfully –
in a tunnel of silence. Every real poem is the breaking of
an existing silence, and the first question we might ask
any poem is, what kind of voice is breaking silence,
and what kind of silence is being broken?
– *Adrienne Rich*

*Migritude breaks silences – personal, familial, global, historical. Each poem
in this section was born of migrant journeys: my physical, transcontinental
migrations; my creative evolution from poet to performer; my internal shift
from self-protective silence to political expression.*

*Some of the poems – "Eater of Death," for example, and "Notes From A
Lost Country" – were included in earlier drafts of the performance script,
but got dropped in the final cut. "The Making" was written at 3am. I had
just committed to creating the show, and woke nightly in a cold sweat
over everything I didn't know, all the skills and resources I didn't have,
the gut terror of not knowing what I was doing.*

These poems laid the groundwork for Migritude.

OPENING

To reach the depth of the soul, that which is unmanifest,
we need to be totally open to great joy without attachment.
– Ligia Dantes

what would it take
to let joy go
with the same wide arms
that drew it in?

willingness to be a flute
hollow open at both ends
trusting the power
and range of its voice
when the gathered breath
strikes the waiting
space within

RELEASE

I will give myself to the dance,
no longer the dancer,
    give myself to the poem,
no longer the poet,
    burn myself in the fire,
no longer the kindler

Who's watching
    hide
Who's watching
    freeze
They're watching
He's watching
She's watching
    get off the stage

I will give myself
to the moment
    not the thought
give myself to the story
    not the reception
bow down to the gods
    not the applause

Who's watching now
    everyone
Who's watching now
    no one
Who's watching now
    me

What if they laugh
laugh with them
What if they leave
have faith
What if they hate me
love them
and be true to your story

Are they watching
they are watching
Are you watching
I am watching
Who are they
Who are you
we are all the truth
inside your story

WHAT WE KEEP

I.
Ben, my eldest aunt
asks in the morning:
What would you like for dinner?
Puri and keri no rus?
But you don't eat fried food.

Ben hasn't slept all night:
sciatica, fibromyalgia,
osteoarthritis, osteoporosis.
When she was 34
doctors in Nairobi
scooped out her ovaries,
uterus, fallopian tubes
like seeds from a pawpaw;
why would she want them
anymore? She had three sons.

At the age of 34,
Ben entered menopause,
her bones began to thin.
Now a slip fractures her femur
or hip, a vigorous cough or sneeze
splinters her ribs.

II.
At 5 pm she takes the can
of mango pulp from fridge.
Ratna, she shows me.
The best kind to buy
if you're not going to make it

from fresh mangoes.
Puts a folded dishcloth
on the counter.
The can on the dishcloth.
Opens drawer.
Hands me can opener.
I'm too weak to do this now.

He mara prabhu, oh my Lord,
visit this pain on no one else.

I open the can. She puts out a dish.
I pour orange pool of mango pulp.
I reach for spoon to scrape the can.
No, she pulls out rubber spatula,
shows me with shaking hands
how to get each last drop.

She needs to rest now.
Fans her face, pants
on her recliner.

I take her foot between my hands
Ben, shall I cut your toenails?

They are long, jagged, yellow.
Her face melts with embarrassment.

I do one each day. It's too hard
to bend over longer than that.
We came into this world
with just our bodies
and even those
we'll have to leave
when we go.

we don't our bodies are borrowed vessels, holding in and protecting our souls

III.
At 6pm she heats the oil.
I've made the puri dough.
She shows me how to test
the heat of the oil
with a crumb of dough.
I roll out puris
try to get them round.
Don't worry about
size and shape,
just do your best.

Mine are shaped like countries.
Kenya. England. India. America.

We have traveled half the world
with hearts open,
we've seen everything.
Always remember who we are,
where we came from,
and you'll never do evil.

She shows me how to slip them
into the oil smooth side down,
so they swell perfectly.

No one in America knows
how to make good puris.

She lays an old towel on the floor,
in front of the cooker,
to catch spills.
Opens out six sheets of newspaper
with kitchen towel on top
for the oil-crisp puris.

Koi bhija ne na dhyo, prabhu,
she murmurs
Give this pain to no one else.

IV.
She points out the shine
of oil still left
in the pan I washed,
the splashes around the sink.
No Zen master
could be more exacting.

I'm training you.
You left home so long ago
and you've lived anyhow since then,
don't feel bad when I correct you.

Later a glass slips from my hand
shatters on the floor.

Never mind bete,
even people die,
why should we expect
a poor glass to live forever?

life is a gift, purchased
with your mother's
pain and father's
delight/pleasure
A gift that doesn't
last forever. wear
and tear wear and
down a body and
tears down life

PLEASE DO NOT TOUCH

Some day I'll start a museum
where all Works Of Art
are for touching:

itchy fingers can sink
into sculptures stroke
grained canvasses trace
calligraphy
on manuscripts

hands can swell
with contours corners

where you can sniff
Art if you choose
wrap arms
around it roll it

across the floor bite
into Art if so moved
kick a piece
that triggers rage dismember
what provokes and lick
the Works that unleash joy

Art that stays intact
will be retired

don't be
afraid to live
pain is part of life,
discomfort is a part of
life. if all you do is nothing
then nothing will
become of you.

EATER OF DEATH

Based on the true story of Bibi Sardar, whose husband and
seven children were killed at breakfast by US air strikes on
Kabul in October 2001. To date, over ten thousand Afghani
civilians have been killed by US military action.

I.
They came as we ate breakfast, I remember the taste
of black market naan.
Zainab and Shahnaz turned eyes like whirlpools
as I sprinkled them
with precious water.
My children ate slowly,
tasting each crumb.
I remember the bitterness
in my throat.

Before we finished
the sky ripped open, vomited
death, everything
fell, burned,
a voice like a jackal's howled
Kamal Gohar Shahnaz
Sadiyah Zainab Zarafshan

On and on, after all
the other noises
stopped
Kamal Gohar Shahnaz Sadiyah Zainab Zarafshan
split my head, I would have beaten it
into silence.

I raised my hands

to block my ears, my fingers fell
into the well
of a hole in my face,
the howling
came from me.

II.
Three days later,
in the shelter,
starvation and nausea
fought in my gut.
Aziza, my neighbour,
shards of rubble
still in her matted hair,
showed me
a package. Yellow
like the bombs. With an
American flag.
They say it's food.

Her mouth twitched, her head jerked,
her one remaining hand shook, spittle and words
jumped from her lips:
Food coloured like
the bombs. For the children
still alive
to pick from minefields
with the hands
they still have left.

And finally
I saw
the savagery
of a people

who would gloat
over those they kill.
I cried out
to the shelter roof:
Have they no mothers
no children
in Amrika?

III.
On the ninth day,
after Aziza died
still clutching the pack
she refused to open, I
pried it from her lifeless
lacerated fingers, I

ate the food.

The blood and bones and fat
of my children,
in a yellow pack,
with an Amrikan flag.

I ate the names
I'd patted into my belly
as they ripened inside me,
one by one. The names
that angered
their father, who said
in his despair:

What future have they
in this country that's meat
for wolves?

I answered him:

Each of them
is a miracle of life, I will not
dim their wonder.

Kamal – perfection, how you bruise
and scrape my abscessed tongue.
Gohar – diamond, precious stone,
now break my loosened teeth.
Shahnaz – princess, red gelatinous heart
of this monstrous American pastry,
I smear you on my mouth.
Sadiyah – blessed one, sink in my stomach,
stone of my womb, I take you back.
Zainab – granddaughter of the Prophet, peace
be unto him, and you, sugar
my saliva, prophesy
what comes to eaters of death.
Zarafshan –
Zar-af-shan, littlest one, I named you
for a mighty river. You taste now
of rancid mud, you taste now
of poisoned fish,
littlest one
you taste
of splintered glass.

IV.
Their names will not be remembered,
They are not *Amrikan.*
Museums will not hold their relics, they are not
Amrikan. No other mother's
children will be slaughtered

in their memory, they are not
Amrikan.

But I? I have eaten
from the bowels of hell,
chewed and swallowed
the fragments of my children
and now
do you see?

Seal the borders
of my body to pain,
seal my eyes, mouth, belly
to any hunger not
my own. I rename myself
Amrika. No love
no grief in the world but mine.

And I will keep them safe –
in the cracks of my teeth
in the pit of my pelvis
in the raw raw flesh
beneath my eyelids.

Kamal
Gohar
Shahnaz
Sadiyah
Zainab
Zarafshan

NOTES FROM A LOST COUNTRY

*make tea not war make friends not war make gazpacho
not war make saag paneer not war make me a channel of
your peace not war make eggs*
— From the window of my local tapas joint

Day 1 and 2 of Operation Shock And Awe | protestors
pack dowtown by day, helicopters | circle relentless by
night. Until 4am, a flock | of roaring metal fists. Sleep
impossible | despite earplugs. Later, I hear | only one
'copter was police. | The rest were media piranhas.
Seeking flesh | for "Anarchy In San Francisco" headlines.

Snapshot 1: | Anarchy in San Francisco. | 8am, Market
Street, at Beale. | 7 activists do yoga asanas on the
concrete pavement. Beautiful | as dancers. Radiance |
that draws a suit | to down his briefcase | join. Awkward.
Stiff.

Facing them | a row of cops. Full riot gear. | Heavy boots
thick | ugly jackets belts bristling | with weapons. They'd
be ludicrous | if they weren't menacing. | If we hadn't
seen | the clubs and kicks and blows | on unarmed flesh.

Snapshot 2: Anarchy | in San Francisco. | Lunchtime.
Market and Main. | Cops haul limp resistors | out of
junction. Six police | to each protestor. Cops | fence
us in on pavement | over a hundred cops shoulder | to
shoulder all the way | to Embarcadero.

A female Asian officer | stands before me. Young. | Our
faces level. No–eye–contact | gun-fat-on-hip club-at-
ready | legs-apart-boots-planted. | Behind her 4 cops

carry a protestor / to police van. I lean forward / eyes strain to record – one foot / touches road. Her club arm body / swing at me. *GET BACK.*

I've been waiting days to cry. / Now before this Asian woman / Officer I. Michaud, SFPD #915 / I cry. Stand. Breathe. / Cry.

Workplace conversation, Day 2 of the war: / "Are you all right?" / "No. Four million pounds / of bombs are falling on Iraq." / "Boy, you're not much fun today." / Did anyone have to explain not being fun / on 9/11?

Palpable bewilderment / of Pentagon, plaintive wail of playground bully: "They weren't supposed / to fight back!"

Dispatch, 1897, from Commander / Jackson, British Army in Kenya. On resistance of Nandi people / to British invasion: *"...the ignorance / of the people is so extreme / that it is impossible to convey / to such savages that the occupation of their country / is not harmful to them..."*

Op-Ed, Kenya's *Daily Nation*: "Pray / That Kenya Never Discovers / Oil."

"I want to do a Rip Van Winkle," / I tell my lover. / "Wake me in a hundred years / if anything's better. If not, don't bother." / "Poor baby," he responds. / "You need to drink more coffee."

Chant for the dead and dying / for the screaming survivors / *Sarvesham shantir bhavatu* / may peace be unto all / *Sarvesham purnam bhavatu* / may wholeness be unto all / May all be free of sorrow / pain / may all look to the good of others.

Chant to hold breath / to soul, gut / to breath, heart / to gut, brain / to breathing heart.

FIRST DATES IN UTOPIA

In this room, for one hour
let's be easy in our skins
observe ourselves
with gentle curiosity
proffer and accept
selected morsels of our lives.

Let's regard each other
with eyes that smile
with faces that engage,
savor without urgency
the strangeness of being human.

LOVE POEM FOR LONDON

The night Youssou N'Dour
sang at the South Bank
cicadas shrieked for joy
in Stockwell's streets
gargoyles jumped off Westminster Abbey
to bump and grind in alleyways.

The night Ravi Shankar
played sitar at Albert Hall
queer Asian boys with kohl-rimmed eyes
danced bhangra in the lanes of Brixton
saffron sashes at their wrists and hips.

The night the Japanese theatre company
played A Midsummer Night's Dream
in the shadow of St. Paul's Cathedral
boneless Tokyo acrobats
cartwheeled across Covent Garden
Oberon and Titania swept the Strand
in satin kimono embroidered like gardens
Helena wept exquisite porcelain tears
into the Thames.

Fairies donkeys
gamboled the Embankment
whispered into autumn wind
if we spirits have offended
think but this and all is mended
if we spirits have offended......

You kissed frangipani
round my wrists

I planted Nandi flame
along your spine
jasmine bloomed
beneath my skin
under your lips.

We leapt for red buses
flew into windstreams
gravity-free
bodies spun midair.

The night voices of Senegal
ran molten gold into the Thames
speedboats turned to clove-laden dhows
trade winds belled their sails
ice cubes clinked into cowrie shells
across the city's wine bars.

The night the edges of London
flowed out to passionate raags
silver anklets on disembodied feet
jingled dandia rhythms
down Whitehall.

Police truncheons fruited nectarines
tear gas canisters burped out
green coriander clouds
Hyde Park squirrels flashed neon orange
tree to tree like northern lights
banana trees exploded
greenhouse walls in Kew
coffee bushes flung
red berries to the swans.

We feasted on falafel in Trafalgar Square
sitting on bronze lions under Nelson's stare
cars a crazy headlamp-dance around our centrifuge.

You said
Paris?
I said
Forget it
you offered the Seine
I said
French nuclear tests in the Pacific
you whispered
Champs Elysees
I snarled
racist visa policies
you murmured
Provence
I said
Jean Le-Pen
you painted romance
I parried
with politics.

We were both right
and we were both wrong
making a poem
we hadn't a shape for
layering improvised harmonies
onto an unscored page.

You licked houmous
off my fingers
which is one way
to win an argument.

N'dour sang richest red
laterite dust
into our nostrils
Shankar silvered nets of raags
around the shoals of London boroughs
stockbrokers stirred
in brandied dreams
woke to sandalwood crumbs
rain-insect wings
on their pillows.

The night Shakespeare's midsummer madness
became forever Japanese
Puck backflipped
through bush through briar
heartbreak and truth
through flood through fire
illusion and mischief
I do wander everywhere
swifter than a moon's sphere.

We all served the fairy queen that night.
London lay at our feet
Omani carpet Kashmiri shawl
symphony we entered
your woodwind my percussion
story with a subplot
shaped exactly like us.

I was electric, you incandescent.
My hair shot sparks, your breath ignited.

THE MAKING

Make it out of the sari that wraps you / in tender
celebration / like the mother you longed for / make it out
of the mother you got / in all her wounded magnificence

Make it out of every scar and callus / on your father's
hands / and how you always wanted / tough mechanic's
hands like his / credentialled by each ground-down
fingernail each / palm line seamed with grease

Distill it from the offering / of his hands / to fifty years
of labour to guarantee / that his daughters would never
have to work with theirs

Make it / to find out / what your own hands are good for

Make it of all the hands that have ever / touched you
the hand that grabbed your eighteen-year-old breast /
on a Nairobi street / so that weeks after / you still walked
hunched over / arms against chest / the hands that slid
a needle into your inner elbow / drew up a fat column
of liquid red to test if it was / pure enough to get you a
green card / hands that taught you how to throw / elbow
strikes pull / mouth-rips hands / that sing healing into
your muscles hands / that have worshipped you / in ways
that leave you / consecrated / humbled

Make it for the hands / hacked off the Arawaks by
Columbus and his men / lopped off Ohlone children by
the Spanish priests / baskets of severed hands presented
at day's end / to Belgian plantation masters in the Congo
thumbs / chopped off Indian weavers by the British /
make it because you / still have hands

Make it for everyone / who's ever said / *You think too*
hard you talk / too much you question / more than you need to
you're too / intense too serious you're too / angry / lighten UP
for chrissake it's not like YOU / have family in Eye-rak!

Make it because you don't have / health insurance / it
flashes neon in your brain / each time you take a fall
in dance class / ride a road without a bike lane / your
close friend / is fifty-three she has no / health insurance
it would cost her / four hundred dollars a month / when
you think / about health insurance you remember zari /
threads of beaten silver woven into saris so that in
extremity / a woman could burn her saris / recover
the molten silver / you wonder how it feels to touch a
lighted match / to your inheritance

Make it because Iraqis / had free healthcare one of the
world's best / before the US invasion / now / children
scream ceaselessly four or five to a bed from the pain /
of sand parasites for want of / three cents worth of
antibiotics / women give birth on the floor / in corners
not packed with war victims

Make it for every morning you've ever / opened your eyes
to the luminous beauty of a lover's sleeping face /
known with every cell of your body / that life is joy /
make it for times you've prayed to die to silence /
screams you can no longer bear to hear / make it because
you have never feared / death / only the pain of living
with eyes wide open

Make it with your body / pain in your shoulders / numb and
tingle of your carpal tunnel hands ice / in your toes each
morning chant / of your feet laughter / of your hips on the
dance floor conversation / of your pelvis / with mortality

Make it from rage / every smug idiotic face you've
ever wanted to smash / into the carnage of war every
encounter / that's left your throat choked / with what
you dared not say excavate / the words that hid in your
churning stomach through visa controls / words you
swallowed down / until over the border they are / still
there they knew / you would return for them

Make it knowing that art / is not political change / make
it a prayer / for real political change / a homage to your
heroes a libation / to your gods

Make it for the archaic meaning / of the word maker /
poet / for the Greek root / of the word poet / to create

Make it to surrender the delusion / that you are creator
that you do anything other / than get yourself out of
the way / for this juggernaut of silk and woven power /
this tapestry of blood and history

Because you never know enough / but you can learn /
you'll never be / ready but you can fake it / because the
when and where / are here and now the answers / to who
and what / are you and this the how / and why / will
reveal themselves / in the making.

Because ready / is never a question just a reminder / to
breathe / and jump

IV.

THE JOURNEY

Sarva aarambhaa hi doshena dhoomena agni iva aavruta.
Beginnings are imperfect,
like the smoke fire releases before it burns.

—SANSKRIT PROVERB

Migritude is political history told through personal story. It is also the tale of a creative journey. The timeline in this section seeks to capture both. The choice of what to include and leave out was somewhat idiosyncratic. I wanted to show that Empires reproduce themselves; that history buried becomes history repeated; that art is as much process as product. That we cannot know ourselves or our nations – or meet the truth of our present moment – until we look at how we got here.

MIGRITUDE TIMELINE

6th Century BCE   Earliest depictions of boteh / ambi /
                    paisley motif in Central Asia.

Common Era Begins

800 - 1500   Flourishing Indian Ocean Trade
                    between inland African Kingdoms,
                    East Africa Coast, Arabian Peninsula,
                    India, and SE Asia. Evolution of
                    Swahili language, a mixture of Arabic,
                    Indian, and Bantu languages.

1600   British East India Company awarded
                    charter to trade in India.

1757   India becomes Crown Colony.

1788   African Association formed in England
                    to explore the interior of Africa.

1813   Britain imposes 80% duty on Indian
                    textile exports.

1816 - 1818   Shaka comes to power as Zulu King and
                    forms Zulu kingdom.

1846   Kashmir annexed and sold by Britain.

1884 - 1885   Fourteen European countries attend
                    Berlin Conference, divide Africa
                    between them by drawing lines across
                    a map of the continent.

1887	British East Africa Company awarded charter to trade.
1893	Creation of East African Protectorate over area that roughly approximates present-day Kenya.
1895 - 1902	32,000 indentured Indian labourers imported by British to build East African railway. About 2,300 die during their contracts.
1905 - 1907	Maji Maji uprising in Tanzania against German occupation.
1920	British East African Protectorate becomes Crown Colony, renamed Kenya. Indian indentured labour ends in Kenya. About 6,700 Indians choose to stay in Kenya to work as shopkeepers, artisans, clerks, and administrators.
1920 - 1948	More Indians migrate to East Africa.
1947	India wins independence.
1952 - 1959	Mau Mau freedom fight in Kenya. State of emergency and gulag imposed by British colonial government. Idi Amin serves in colonial regiment, the King's African Rifles, whose soldiers incarcerate, torture, and murder Kenyans in concentration camps.

1963	Kenya wins independence. British army continues to send 3,000 soldiers a year to Kenya for training at 5 military ranges.
1965	Rapes of Kenyan women by British soldiers. These continue for 35 years, until 2001. Injuries to local communities from unexploded bombs and ammunition on their land.
1966	Opposition parties banned. Kenya becomes single-party state.
1971	Idi Amin seizes power in Uganda in a military coup backed by Britain, Israel, the US, and apartheid South Africa.
1972	Idi Amin expels Uganda's 80,000 Asians, seizes their assets.
1980 - 1982	Volcker Shock creates Third World Debt Crisis. Followed by IMF-imposed structural adjustment programme, which eliminates Kenya's public healthcare and public education, and creates ever-intensifying economic hardship for the next two decades.
1982	Abortive military coup in Kenya. In the aftermath, my family is sponsored for immigration to the US by aunt who lives there.

1996	I receive my papers to immigrate to the US. Backpack around the country for six months. Get my first check for a poem.
1991	Opposition parties unbanned in Kenya, but state repression of dissent continues.
2002	Ruling party KANU defeated in general election by NARC Rainbow coalition of opposition parties. Twenty-four-year tyranny of Daniel Arap Moi ends. I complete "Shilling Love." I protest Gulf War II (Shock and Awe). Kenyan pastoralists win $7 million in legal case against the British Ministry of Defense for injuries from unexploded bombs and ammunition left by British Army on local land.
2003	Kenyan survivors of rape by British soldiers begin legal action against Britain's Ministry of Defense. I am laid off from my job, become a full-time artist.
2004	I meet Kim Cook, germinate the concept of *Migritude* as spoken-word theatre.
2005	Work-in-progress performances of *Migritude* in Berkeley and LA.
2006	Work-in-progress performances in Vienna, Zanzibar, Rome, New York. I take *Migritude* home to Kenya. Full show premieres in Berkeley and San Francisco.

2007	*Migritude* gets standing ovation at World Social Forum, Nairobi. Full run of show in Nairobi and Mombasa. Featured on *SPARK! Arts and Culture* on KQED TV in its season premiere, "Patel, Ferlinghetti, and Guidi."
2008	New legal case initiated in Kenya on rape allegations against British Army soldiers. Excerpts of *Migritude* presented in Zimbabwe, South Africa, Italy. LietoColle publishes a bilingual Italian-English edition of the stage-script of *Migritude* that is launched at the International Poetry Festival in Genoa, a port city of migrants.
2009	Mau Mau veteran survivors and Kenya Human Rights Commission file suit in the British High Court for reparations from the British government for torture. LietoColle edition of *Migritude* is shortlisted for the Camaiore International Poetry Prize.
2010	Kenya passes a new constitution by a 70% majority in a national referendum. The constitution guarantees the rights envisioned at independence for all Kenyans, including women and minorities.
October 2010	*Migritude* published by Kaya Press.

A good interview, like a good poem, throws up surprises and discoveries for its participants as well as its readers. Conversation can bring into being ideas not fully articulated before. With the best interviews, as with the best poems, I find at the end that I'm somewhere different from where I started – a place I had no idea I was heading. My work reveals a new layer of its personality to me.

Emanuele Monegato has never seen Migritude *performed. He first encountered the work in book form, as the Italian / English edition published by Italian poetry press, LietoColle.*

ON *MIGRITUDE*:
A CONVERSATION WITH
SHAILJA PATEL
By Emanuele Monegato

Shailja Patel is the author of *Migritude*, "a meditation about the processes of colonialism and postcolonialism, especially as they unfolded in Kenya, her native land." In addiction to her Kenyan origin, all of Patel's cultural backgrounds are to be found in her work: the fact of being a South Asian brought up in Kenya, an Indian student in England, and a woman of colour in the United States merge into her blank verses, giving shape to the peculiar oeuvre that is *Migritude*.

In Italy, Patel has performed *Migritude* since 2006. In 2008, the publishing house LietoColle published an English/Italian version of the work in a translation by Marta Matteini and Pina Piccolo.

E. Monegato: *I will start our interview with a peculiar question: which is your own relationship with questions and interviews? I am asking it because in "The Making/Migrant Song" you state that: "We absorb information without asking questions, because questions can be dangerous. Can make us stand out, cost us jobs, visas, lives. We watch and copy. We try to please."*

S. Patel: Those lines refer to the risks involved for migrants, or outsiders of any kind, when they ask questions. My relationship to being questioned depends entirely on the purpose of the questioning, and the framework of reference from which the questions come. I get impatient with questions which are ill-informed, or don't recognize the questioner's prejudices. I deeply appreciate questions which open up new ideas for me, and new readings of my work.

E. Monegato: *I first got in touch with* Migritude *during a Translation Studies Seminar when Marta Matteini, one of its two Italian translators, started quoting the following verse: "If we cannot name it does it exist?" Can you comment upon this?*

S. Patel: That line is from the poem "Dreaming In Gujarati." I am exploring the idea that language defines our reality and lived experience. If we don't have a word for something, it doesn't inform our collective reality.

E. Monegato: *"Language is power" is a well-known motto. You once answered a question about your favourite language stating that "Poetry is the world's most beautiful language." Do you think we can melt these two sentences and state that "Poetry is power"?*

S. Patel: I would say, rather, that language is a tool. Like any tool, its power depends on the skill with which it is wielded, and the choice of the right words for the right moment, used in the most effective way. Poetry, at its best, is a distillation of language and perception to its purest, most intelligent and powerful essence.

E. Monegato: *How much of the political involvement shown in your performance of "Eater of Death" could be found in* Migritude?

S. Patel: Migritude unfurls the voices of women living in the bootprint of Empire. "Eater of Death" is the story of one such woman – an Afghani woman who lost her entire family to US bombs. "Eater of Death" was actually a part of earlier drafts of *Migritude*, and then cut out when my director and I made an editorial decision to focus on women in East Africa. *Migritude* is unabashedly political – feminist and anti-imperialist.

E. Monegato: *In "Idi Amin" you alternate between the history of official facts ("This is the history I learned in school. Standard 3 – 5, Hospital Hill Primary School, Nairobi.") and that of personal stories ("This is the history we didn't learn."). This alternation could be considered one of the key features of* Migritude. *What is the importance given to history in your life and how does it interact with your own activism as a female writer?*

S. Patel: History buried becomes history repeated. A whole generation of Africans have been denied the truth of their own history, and so we do not really know ourselves, or our countries. Reclaiming those erased or hidden histories is vital political and creative work, and is central to my purpose as a writer.

E. Monegato: *In one of your interviews published by* Legendaria *you affirm that sometimes you feel like a translator because you forge into poetry facts, data and figures, colonialism and post-colonialist views. As such, I would like to ask you about the importance of the Italian translation of* Migritude. *Don't you think that such a translation could be seen as a migration of contents, behaviours, thoughts, and stories?*

S. Patel: Art is a migrant – it travels from the vision of the artist to the eye, ear, mind and heart of the listener. Translation adds another layer to the migration, is another leg of the journey.

E. Monegato: *After having read your work I still have problems in finding a proper definition for it. "Performance poetry," "spoken-word poetry," "fragments," and "poetic vignettes" are all words that could be used to describe* Migritude. *In my humble opinion, they are all reductive and simplistic if considered one by one. The only way to portray* Migritude *is to use a net of definitions describing its multiple souls. How do you normally define your work?*

S. Patel: Poetry. Spoken-word theatre. Text-based performance for stage. Fully embodied poetry. Story! I like the description "multiple souls." What I do breaks new ground in melding genres and dissolving boundaries – it is fluid, multifaceted, and constantly evolving.

This interview was originally published in *Altre Modernità* (Other Modernities), the journal of the Cultural Studies section of Università degli Studi di Milano.

Monegato, Emanuele. (2009). *"On Migritude Part 1:
When Saris Speak – The Mother. A Conversation with Shailja Patel." /Altre Modernità*, 0 /(2). http://riviste.unimi.it/index.php/AMonline/article/view/300/422 (16 August 2010)

Vanita Reddy came to the world premiere of Migritude *in Berkeley, CA with no previous knowledge of my work. She was writing her PhD dissertation on Indian femininities, and the sari theme in* Migritude *caught her attention. Having seen the work performed and embodied, her questions probe my performance of identity, culture, and gender – the politics of my sari-wrapped body.*

COME FOR THE SARIS,
STAY FOR THE POLITICS:
AN INTERVIEW WITH SHAILJA PATEL
By Vanita Reddy

Vanita Reddy: *I had the pleasure of seeing your show at the*
La Peña Cultural Center in November 2006. I also have a
DVD of your performance in San Francisco. I was struck by
one of the anecdotes posted on your blog. You were attending
ArtWallah in L.A. and were getting mehndi on your back.
You wrote that you wanted people to "come for the saris and
stay for the politics" or "come for the mehndi and stay for
the migritude." It was that catchphrase that drew me to the
show, in fact. What do you mean by that catchphrase?

Shailja Patel: One of the challenges of my work is how
to draw mainstream audiences who wouldn't normally
be interested in "political theatre." So those phrases are
half-satirical: they're referencing the marketing value of
"exotic" images that will attract audiences. And they're
half-serious: the saris, the mehndi, are the containers of
history, politics, economics, woven into fabric, codified
into shape and pattern.

V. Reddy: *Why do you use saris to "speak" the story of*
migrancy, especially the story of migration from East Africa?
In a related question, you describe Migritude *as an attempt*
to make "intimate family treasures public" (saris, jewellery,
etc.). What meaning do these objects hold for you? What
motivated your decision to display them in the show?

S. Patel: My mother has been collecting saris and
jewellery for me since I was a child, to give to me as my
trousseau when I married. A few years ago, she gave up
on me getting married anytime soon, and decided it was

time to give me my trousseau regardless. So I received this red suitcase packed with exquisite saris, this jewellery that had been kept safe for over 30 years for me. There were no occasions or events in my daily life as an artist/activist in the Bay Area where I could use or wear these items. I felt enormously guilty that they were just sitting there, gathering dust.

So I came up with the idea of using them in my work. At first, I thought about a gallery exhibition, where they would be displayed alongside poems that explored their history and meaning. Then I met my director Kim Cook, who suggested that we use them in a one-woman show I wanted to do, which would tell untold stories of colonialism and imperialism, through the lens of the South Asian Diaspora.

V. Reddy: *In an interview I heard on NPR you noted that you have vexed relationship to saris, that you had preconceptions about feeling "exotic" and/or "weak" in them. Can you say more about why you felt (or feel) this way?*

S. Patel: The piece in Act I of the show, "Swore I'd Never Wear Clothes I Couldn't Run Or Fight In" lays out all the messages I received as a girl, about wearing a sari, about femininity, about the sari-draped body.

When I left home, and lived in the UK and the US, I encountered Western stereotypes about women in saris. Both orientalist – Indian women in saris are exotic, mysteriously alluring, sexy, mystical – and racist/ sexist – Indian women in saris must be oppressed, uneducated, un-cosmopolitan, not fluent in English.

V. Reddy: *Related to this, you describe that when*

photographed with mehndi on your hand, "I make sure my
fist is clenched. I don't want any of the images to slot into
convenient fetishized stereotypes of Indian women." What
does the clenched fist represent to you?

S. Patel: A reclaiming of voice, of power. The "migrant attitude" captured in the word "migritude": the voice of a generation of migrants who speak unapologetically, fiercely, lyrically, for themselves.

V. Reddy: *Your website defines "migritude" in part as a reassertion of the "dignity" of outsider status in its play on "négritude" and "attitude." How do you see these terms working in your show?*

S. Patel: On how "négritude" works in the show, a friend of mine, Jiwon Chung, a director and teacher of Boal's Theater of the Oppressed, captured it better than I can. He writes:

> "It shares the richness of connotation and inspiration of négritude, as applied to immigrants: a celebration and revalorization of immigrant/diasporic culture and identity, its greatness 'measured by the compass of suffering' (Aimé Césaire), with overtones of spiritual and political liberation.

> "It's also powerful because it has the arresting, corruscating, academic luster of a freshly minted neologism, but also has harsher/oppressed undertones of 'nigger', 'meager/maigre', 'magreb/maigreb (North African colonies)'. It starts out (in French) with a tonal and somatic sense of contraction followed by an enlongated, large,

expansive, inclusive reprieve. 'Tude, Attitude,
Gratitude, Lattitude, Beatitude."

The show is packed with "attitude" – both in content
and delivery. As a performer and writer, I'm saying: *My
job is not to make you feel good. My job is to crack open your
complacency, show you what you've chosen not to see, make
you squirm.*

V. Reddy: *What is your relationship, if any, to key players in
the négritude movement, such as Césaire and Senghor?*

S. Patel: Césaire and Senghor are not direct influences
or primary sources for *Migritude*. But the political and
cultural space they opened up through négritude, and
the discourse that continues from that, were the soil in
which *Migritude* could germinate.

V. Reddy: *Your website describes you as a "Kenyan,"
and in other places (books that anthologize your poetry,
for example), you've been described as "Kenyan-Indian-
American." What is your relationship to these definitions of
your identity? Is there a term or descriptor that you prefer,
and if so, why?*

While I can understand the need people have to label,
I find labels and identities of minimal use. So I correct
obvious factual errors – for example, when I'm described
as "Indian" in Kenya, or Africa, I always correct that by
pointing out that I am actually a Kenyan, or African, of
Indian heritage. But to me, what really defines a person
is what they DO, not what ethnicity / nationality / racial
identity they claim.

I take June Jordan's position: "I will call you my brother,

I will call you my sister, on the basis of what you do
for justice, what you do for equality, what you do for
freedom, and not on the basis of who you are." And
Edward Said's, who wrote that he experiences himself as
a confluence of tides, or currents, a sea of moving selves,
rather than a fixed "identity."

V. Reddy: *In an article in* Nirali *magazine published in
October 2006, the writer described your shifting identities
in this way: "As a South Asian growing up in Kenya, a South
Asian student in England, and now a woman of color in the
United States, Patel knows all about living as an outsider."
Do you consider yourself a "woman of color" in the United
States? In what ways do you—or don't you—align yourself
with, say, women of color feminists such as Cherrie Moraga,
Gloria Anzaldua, etc.?*

S. Patel: *This Bridge Called My Back* was a major influence
for me, as it was for a whole generation of young
feminists of color. It gave me language and conceptual
tools for my experience. Yes, I do consider myself a
woman of color in the US, because that is the first line of
perception I encounter when I walk down the street.

V. Reddy: *I see several quotes by Arundhati Roy on your
website. Is she a role model of sorts for you? What is your
relationship to her work?*

S. Patel: Absolutely. I love her work. I've said on my blog
that: "Everything Arundhati Roy writes, reads like a love
poem to me. She does not separate her heart from her
politics. Her humanity from her brilliance and piercing
analysis."

V. Reddy: *There is only one point in the show that you say the* word "lesbian" out loud, and it's toward the end, when you describe "don't exist in Gujarati: / Self-expression / Individual / Lesbian." Why did you decide to group "lesbian" with these other terms?

S. Patel: Because it symbolizes the way in which a language – in this case, Gujarati – can erase a person, by not having a word for who they are.

V. Reddy: *As I noted earlier, I "came for the saris, and stayed for the politics," in part because of my own identification as a diasporic Indian woman. Who do you imagine as your audience for* Migritude? *Specifically, to what extent are you targeting Indian diasporic audiences by telling the story of* Migritude *with saris? Or is there a different audience that you have in mind?*

As an artist, I want my work to reach everyone in the world, because I believe it has something to say to everyone in the world! From a marketing point of view, of course we begin by targeting audiences who are likely to relate to the themes – migrants, women, members of the South Asian and African diasporas.

What I have learned from touring my work internationally, however, is never to make assumptions about who my "target audience" should be. I have found that the work genuinely crosses all boundaries of race, gender, culture, and even language.

The most telling example of this is that the book of *Migritude* has been published in Italy, and translated into Italian. At the book launch in Genoa, the owner of the bookshop where we did the launch (a male Italian scientist) said how powerfully the poems spoke to his own experience of growing up in Calabria, an economically marginalized region of Italy. How could I ever have imagined that?

ACKNOWLEDGMENTS

*[I]t took a global conspiracy to make this book.
I'm so fortunate to have been supported by this
amazing web of humanity.*
– Naomi Klein, *The Shock Doctrine*

MIGRITUDE THEATRE PRODUCTION

Migritude had its World Premiere on November 5th, 2006, at La Peña Cultural Centre, Berkeley, CA.

Migritude was co-commissioned by La Peña Cultural Center in partnership with Asian Improv Arts, UC Merced's Art Center Without Walls, and the National Performance Network Creation Fund. The Creation Fund is sponsored by the Doris Duke Charitable Foundation.

Generous support for *Migritude* was provided by the East Bay Community Foundation, the City of Oakland's Cultural Funding Program, the Zellerbach Family Foundation, the William and Flora Hewlett Foundation, Destiny Arts, Iris Arts and Education Group, the Oakland Museum of California, and ODC Theater.

The Kenya Tour of *Migritude* was funded by The Ford Foundation. Thank you Joyce Nyairo and Tade Aina for your faith and investment.

PRODUCTION CREDITS

Kim Cook, DIRECTOR, DRAMATURGE, CO-PRODUCER,
CREATIVE DEVELOPMENT PARTNER.

CHOREOGRAPHER, DANCER: Parijat Desai, www.parijatdesai.org

THE MOTHER (VOICE-OVER RECORDING BY): Vidhu Singh
CONTRIBUTING WRITER: Chandrika Patel

LIGHTING DESIGN: Rachel Vaughn
SOUND ENGINEER: Paris King
MUSIC CREDITS:

> *Ambi / Idi Amin / Maasai Women / Dreaming in Gujarati*
> — Mamuka Berika, Irma Gogiashvili, and
> Robert Rodriguez

> Additional music used in *Idi Amin*
> — "Slideshow 2" by Paris King

> *Shilling Love I & II / Migrant Song*
> — Leland Thunes

> *History Lesson*
> — Drummers of Burundi, from *Spirit of Africa*,
> Real World Records 2001.
> — Yungchen Lhamo from *Fes: The Spirit of Fes 2003*,
> Le Chante du Monde, 2004.

> *Under and Over*
> — "Dolly" and "Miss India" by Riksha,
> from *Your Very Own*, Jhoom Records, 2004.

> *Mangal Sutra*
> — Paris King

IMAGE CREDITS

Aubrey Fagon, www.screenstation.net
Patel Family
Jason Rice, www.jcrice18.com

PUBLICATION CREDITS

Portions of this book were published in the following anthologies, journals, and magazines: *Indivisible: An Anthology of Contemporary South Asian American Poetry*, ed. Bannerjee, Kaippa, and Sundaralingam, University of Arkansas Press, 2010. *Bullets and Butterflies: Queer Spoken Word*, ed. E. Xavier, Suspect Thoughts Press, 2005. *Women's Lives, 3rd , 4th, 5th Editions*, ed. Kirk and Okazawa-Rey, McGraw-Hill, 2003. *Emily Dickinson Award Anthology*, Universities West Press, 2001. *The Literary Review. Chimurenga. The Sow's Ear Poetry Review. Lodestar Quarterly. Kwani?. Tikkun. Trikone Magazine. What If ? - A Journal of Radical Possibilities. Make Magazine. SAMAR (South Asian Magazine for Action and Reflection). Jahazi. Pambazuka News.*

PRODUCTION / BOOK PARTNERS

Wilma Austern, Mamuka Berika, David Borsos, Hina and Jay Bhuva, Jan Camp, Kim Cook, Suhaila Abu Cross, Sarah Crowell, Parijat Desai, Pablo Dosh, Deamer Dunn, Verona Fonte, Philip Gill, Irma Gogiashvili, Fred Hannaham, Annie Leonard, Firoze Manji, Kenny Mostern, AJ Musira, Richie Mwendwa, Chandrika and Narendra Patel, Shruti Patel, Sneha Patel, Mai Palmberg, Ted Plant, Robert Rodriguez, Leland Thunes, Vinay Patel, Indra Mungal, Dunya Ramicova, Leslie Rodd, Shannon Swan, Ali Yahya

DONORS AND CONTRIBUTORS

Anissa Alston, Susan Amrose, Vivek Anand , Naheed
Bardai, Aziz Batada, Frank Baudino, Mandy Benson,
Marnie Berringer, Barbra Blake, Patrick Bond, Evynn
Brezette, Carole Cameron, D. Ross Cameron, Jack Cassetta,
Christine Chai, Jeannine Chapell, Sandra Chatterjee, Paul
Chin, Karen Chow, Derek Chung, Jiwon Chung, Marianne
Clark, Lisa Clayton, Thaddeus Conolly, Natesh Daniel,
Huma Dar, Preethi Desa, Jerry Detry, Lorna Dias, Victor
Dlamini, Meeta and Maneesh Doshi, Adrian D'Souza, Ariel
Dougherty, Phanuel Egejuru, Sarita Evans, Silke Feldman,
Irwin Friedman, Karen Garrett, Richard Gayle, Joel Godiah,
Megan Hanley, Emily & Dave Herbert, Erin Hill, Abdul
Janmohammed, Rahul Joglekar, Sue-Li Jue, Sean Karlin,
Rafique Keshavjee, Vinod and Ajita Khanderia, George
Killeen, Gwyneth Kirk, KRW Printing, Sterling Larrimore,
Diep Le, Daryl Lee, Tom Maliti, Anu Mandavilli, Bill
Mandel, Brinda Moorthy, Nthenya, Tama and Mwendwa
Mule, Vijaya Nagarajan, Anil Naidoo, Lorraine Nelson,
Keith and Cicely Nemitz, Corey Action and Teela Shine
at New Style Motherlode , Michelle Odayaan, Onyango
Oloo, Mahesh Patel, Shanti Perkins, Debra Porter, Vivek
Prabhu, Karthick Ramakrishnan, Rebeca Ramirez-Haskell,
Anita Rao, Madhavi Reddy, Frank Revi, Sean Riley,
Siwaraya Rochanahusdin, Peter and Monica Rorvik, Byron
Rourkacha, Jessica Rucell, Canyon Sam, Sheila Sathe, Susan
Schaller, Junichi Semitsu, Emilio Soldani, Phoebe Ann
Sorgen, Rob Stiles, Tobaji Stuart, Chris Swanson, David
Szlasa, Keith Thomson, Tom Swift, Wangui wa Goro, Tom
Weidlinger, Colleen Wimmer, Tse Sung Wu, Vivian Young,
Linda Zwerdling

For translations and linguistic consultation, deep
appreciation to Bhadra Vadgama and Abdulaziz Lodhi.

Thank you, Claire Light, for envisioning this book, opening

the doors, and invaluable advice on the journey. Sunyoung Lee for making it more, and better. Mayumi Takada for expert editing. Kai-Ming Cha for marketing energy and ingenuity. It has been a delight to work with Chez Bryan Ong, Jen Chou, and Pritsana Kootint-Hadiatmodjo at Spoon and Fork, on the design of this book. Their evolution of a deeply satisfying intertextuality of content with shape, design, colour, and texture, have challenged me to deliver verbal potency that matches the material poetics of the pages.

Thank you, Pina Piccolo and Marta Matteini, for expert translation, the best kind of collaboration, and championing *Migritude* in Italy.

Thank you, Jerry Riley, for the perfect cover image.

Thank you, Emily Taguchi Klingensmith, for bringing *Migritude* to the TV screen. Thank you, Kar Yin Tham and Narissa Lee, for creating a DVD with legs.

Thank you, Cheryl Brown, for wheels, belief, coaching, and celebration.

Lea Arellano, Jan Dederick, Aya De Leon, Lisa Martinovic have had my back and my front throughout the realization of this book. It would not exist without them.

Philo Ikonya and Punam Sood hold me in a thousand ways, across oceans and continents. I am blessed to call them my sisters.

Chris Welch. From the flatworms up.

And finally, LX. For the unconditional faith and support that all artists and writers dream of. For the Room Of One's Own and the tools to use it fully, which make everything else possible.

SHAILJA PATEL was born and raised in Kenya, has lived
in London and San Francisco, and now divides her time
between Nairobi and Berkeley. She honed her poetic skills
in performances that have received standing ovations
throughout Europe, Africa, and North America. She has
been described by the *Gulf Times* as "the poetic equivalent
of Arundhati Roy" and by CNN as "the face of globalization
as a people-centered phenomenon of migration and
exchange." She has appeared on the BBC World Service,
NPR, Al-Jazeera, and her poems have been translated into
twelve languages. She is a recipient of a Sundance Theatre
Fellowship, the Fanny-Ann Eddy Poetry Award from IRN-
Africa, the Voices of Our Nations Poetry Award, a Lambda
Slam Championship, and the Outwrite Poetry Prize. Visit
her at www.shailja.com